THE CHALLENGE
OF THE WORLD
RELIGIONS

THE CHALLENGE
OF THE WORLD
RELIGIONS
GEORG F. VICEDOM

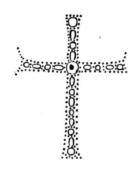

translated by

BARBARA AND KARL HERTZ

FORTRESS PRESS · PHILADELPHIA

Translated from *Die Mission der Weltreligionen* by
Georg F. Vicedom (Munich: Chr. Kaiser Verlag, 1959)
by Barbara and Karl Hertz.

Printed in U.S.A.   UB931

Foreword

We are living in an era marked by possibilities that are cosmic in dimension and events that are unusually significant for the history of ideas. Technology has made it possible for all the peoples of the earth to be in permanent contact with one another and thus also mutually to enrich one another. Involved in a cultural exchange, they are experiencing a fusion of cultures, which has its deepest significance in the influence religions have on one another so as to provide a common spiritual foundation for the community of nations. The present book can offer only a small portion of this enormous process, since it is limited to the phenomenological expression of events in the history of ideas. Its chief concern is to familiarize us Christians with the great task we have in this era. We shall participate in the development of mankind that is coming only to the extent that we seek to mediate to it the best we have, namely, the Gospel. This could be the spiritual contribution which the peoples of Asia and Africa expect from us in the great social revolution in which they are involved. The other religions have recognized that much more is at stake in this than a raising of the standard of living. Will we, also, allow our eyes to be opened? This book wishes at all events to arouse responsibility and to make service a pleasure. I rejoice over the fact that it can appear in an English edition and am grateful to all who have co-operated in its translation and publication.

GEORG F. VICEDOM

Preface

My account of the attack of the world religions upon Christianity* brought to me from various sources the question whether I did not overestimate the propaganda of the world religions. It was said that after the First World War the situation had been similar; the danger had passed. At that time it was actually true that many seeking men turned to the world religions. The church was then, however, in the fortunate position of being stimulated by dialectical theology; in addition, men were captured by a political ideology which pushed aside their religious questions. Today the situation is completely different. Because of the Second World War the religious questions have broken forth more strongly; materialism has brought about a spiritual vacuum; the West has produced no supporting and formative idea; for many men, theology and church have not found the word. In addition there have arisen a number of sects and movements which are deliberately spreading Indic ideas among the nations. The propaganda of the world religions is today no longer carried on by a few educated persons, but is anchored in the conscious sense of mission of peoples who have tens of thousands of their numbers in our territories to study and to learn our technical methods.

The present book wishes, on the one hand, to open the eyes of Christians to what is happening in the area of religion; it wishes to show all who are working for the religious renewal

*Die Weltreligionen im Angriff auf die Christenheit ("Theologische Existenz heute," Neue Folge, Nr. 51 [Munich: Chr. Kaiser, 1956]).

of our people through the Gospel where the questions and the possibilities lie. On the other hand, it wishes to be a help to everyone in confronting the propaganda of the world religions. I therefore chose to let this propaganda speak for itself as much as possible. Thus I have drawn primarily from contemporary material. I did not, to be sure, entirely succeed in dealing with all of this literature. That does not detract from the purpose and claim of this book, since the essential points of view have been so developed that it makes no difference whether one voice more or less is heard.

In the reading of this book, three things should be observed: (1) The book does not concern itself with the religions in their historical form, but with pronouncements which they currently make about themselves. It is therefore not to be expected that we shall find present everywhere the same understanding of themselves which the religions formerly had. (2) The term "Christianity" is used wherever the criticism of the non-Christian religions is directed against the visible forms of the Christian religion. Christianity thus includes the whole complex of "Christian" civilization, culture, and church life. (3) Where the criticism is directed against the message of Christianity, the term "Gospel" is used. On the basis of this Gospel, the spiritual confrontation must be carried out.

The many speeches which I had to give after the appearance of the book mentioned showed me that our congregations would like to get out of the cul-de-sac of Western Christianity. They are allowing the judgments of the other religions upon Christianity to open their eyes to what must be expected of them. I count it as one of the most promising signs of our time that in the great confrontations Christianity lets itself raise questions about its true life and its mandate. The more it attempts to find an answer to these questions, the more God will allow it to sense that blessing which lies in being able to find itself, under the mandate to witness, again a congregation of Jesus.

GEORG F. VICEDOM

viii

Translators' Preface

In this translation we have attempted at all points to remain faithful to the style and content of the original even where we ourselves would have said things differently in English. Every author leaves the marks of his own ways of thinking and of expressing himself on his materials: faithfulness of translation includes communicating these personal qualities as well as the content of the original. It should be noted, however, that the author has approved certain emendations of the original text, and that we have expanded the notes to include some English sources and to provide a frame of reference for the English reader.

Particular attention is drawn to the author's preface in which he points out the sense in which he is using the words "Christianity" and "Gospel." Readers should keep in mind the broad, inclusive, institutional meaning given "Christianity." Although one may distinguish between "Christianity" and "Christendom" in English (as well as in German), the latter term is now relatively rare and tends to carry the meaning which Vicedom assigns to Christianity. For the sake of consistency, therefore, we have used "Christianity" throughout to describe the Christian world as a social organism. We trust this will keep the reader's attention focussed more clearly on the sharply intended distinction between "Christianity" and "Gospel."

BARBARA and KARL HERTZ

Contents

Introduction

From a human point of view the future of Christianity is being decided in Asia today. Its future depends upon the expansion of the Gospel through its missionary effort, upon the missionary zeal of the younger churches, and not least upon the extent to which the world religions are developing their resistance and themselves are becoming missionary religions. Just as the balance of world history is gradually swinging toward Asia, where most of mankind lives, so also the ultimate significance of the Christian church is coming to rest in Asia, even though until now the Christian churches there have been quite weak. It will not depend upon their size, however, but upon their willingness to face up to the non-Christian religions and overcome them. Asia will become an ever stronger factor in the history of the church because a general religious awakening, which is just beginning to manifest itself in Christian territory, is taking place there today. Whether this will benefit the Christian church cannot yet be foreseen. The encounter with the non-Christian religions, however, will take place simultaneously in the Western world because this has now become the mission field of the other religions. These religions offer themselves to Western men as answers to pressing problems, and their solutions are heard, absorbed, and put into practice more widely than we dare admit. Thus these religions have drawn near to us, and today question the intrinsic justification of Christianity. While Christianity previously sought to deal with them without any great observable results, today the world religions have taken the offensive. The great confrontation is now coming and with it comes the real missionary period of Christianity, in which the church must prove the power of its faith and give force to the truth of its message. The other religions view Christianity today as, to say the least, underdeveloped, and they therefore seek to improve it, to rise above it, and to overcome it. Many of us close our eyes to this, not wanting to deal with the real events nor upset the congregations. To do so is to give these religions a free hand and deny the actual missionary command of Christianity. Today, as at all times, the Christian joy in witnessing is the only salvation for the church. This book wishes to help bring this joy into being. When the situation has become such that missionaries of foreign religions travel across the country, when converts to them appear in our colleges, when student congregations can scarcely refute the arguments of Afro-Asian students, and when people argue even in taverns about the "rightness" of religions, then it is time that the church awaken and remember its mandate.

1

The Foundation of the Challenge

1. MISSIONARY MANDATE AND MISSIONARY ZEAL

If today we are confronted with the fact that the world religions, Hinduism, Buddhism and Islam, claim universal validity and carry out a world-wide mission, it is not a result of the political development of the past decade, that is, of the all-determining nationalism in Asia today. Nationalism has only given an added impulse to their missionary zeal. These religions have always contained the claim to universality, even though it has not been apparent in recent times. Since they have no specific structures for religious community, but equate religious community and cultural community, the whole colonial period had to mean for them a defeat of religion, which put them into a kind of narcosis. For them the mastery of the white race, its dominance, was simultaneously a defeat of their gods and a questioning of their religious life. The religions found themselves in a condition of helplessness. Nevertheless, there was ever present in them the awareness of mission, which first made a complete breakthrough when it allied itself with the political goal of freedom. Thus political events released in these religions great spiritual powers by which Christianity finds itself confronted today.

Hinduism

Among the world religions, Hinduism probably has the least missionary zeal. Except for its spread toward Indonesia, it has had no expansion. Nevertheless there lives in it the conviction that its holy writings are inspired and contain the truth for mankind. For its reformers, Ramakrishna, Vivekananda, Gandhi, and Radhakrishnan, Hinduism was the mother of all religions and they did everything to demonstrate that it had a message for mankind. These men viewed the other religions as material for assimilation by Hinduism.[1] Even small sects desired universal recognition: e.g., "that the teaching of Sri Krishna Chaitanya [founder of an Indic sect] shall be proclaimed in every corner and to the ends of the earth."[2] This spirit is widespread in India today. "Hinduism is not a dying religion; its mysteries and its pageantry satisfy the people; its philosophical syncretism appeals to the educated. Ignorance, indifference and pride are the armor against the challenge of the Gospel."[3]

Buddhism

Buddhism has been a missionary religion since its inception. Buddha himself gave his monks and followers the example of the preaching and recruiting missionary. The Buddhist texts are presented mostly in the form of missionary conversations. Buddha lived in the conviction that his teachings and the way to salvation that he had found had meaning for mankind. Therefore he gave his monks a missionary order: "Go ye forth, O Bhikkus [monks], for the gain of the many, for the welfare of the many, in compassion for the world. Proclaim the Doctrine glorious, preach ye

[1] Otto Wolff, *Indiens Beitrag zum neuen Menschenbild: Ramakrishna, Gandhi, Sri Aurobindo* (Hamburg: Rowohlt, 1957), pp. 87–88. See also Hendrik Kraemer, *Religion and the Christian Faith* (London: Lutterworth Press, 1956), p. 134.

[2] B. H. Bon [Bhakti-Hridaya Vana], *My First Year in England: Report of My Activities in the West from May, 1933 to May, 1934* (London, 1934). See also P. D. Devanandan, *The Gospel and Renascent Hinduism* (London: SCM Press, 1959), pp. 52 ff.

[3] Nicolas Zernov, "Christianity in India and the Eastern Orthodox Church," *International Review of Missions* (hereafter referred to as *IRM*), XLIII (1954), 390.

a life of holiness, perfect and pure."[4] And to complete this: "Preach, O Bhikkus, the Dhamma [the eternal law leading to salvation], excellent in the beginning, excellent in the middle, excellent in the end."[5] Even though in Buddhism there have been times of missionary inactivity, in the course of history it has nevertheless succeeded in becoming the religion of choice among the peoples of eastern Asia even though the other religions have continued to exist alongside it. It has become the vehicle of culture of East Asia. Today awakened Buddhism reaches out for all of mankind. It "appears as an evangelizing world religion in the grand manner, such as Christianity. The evangelists of Buddhism, like those of the Christian Gospel, go to all lands. For salvation and redemption shall be proclaimed to all peoples."[6]

The execution of the order to evangelize is today a concern of the Buddhist peoples and gains great momentum from nationalism. The Buddha Jubilee, in particular, called forth a new enthusiasm for evangelism. "It has given an impulse to missionary enterprise among the hill tribes of Burma and Assam and to preaching missions to the West."[7] In a public square in Colombo during the Jubilee years 1954-56, a map of the world was set up with lights at all the places of the world where Buddhism had followers. The people saw in amazement that Buddhism had in fact become a world-wide religion. How great the Buddhists' assurance concerning their mission is, even in the German area, can be seen from the fact that Conze believed he could forego making a German translation of the technical terms, which are difficult to interpret, because they "will probably be assimilated into German speech after a while."[8]

---

[4] Christmas Humphreys, *Buddhism* (Harmondsworth: Penguin Books, 1958), p. 60.

[5] S. Kulandran, *Resurgent Religions* ("World Evangelism Today," No. 1 [London: Lutterworth Press, 1957]), p. 24.

[6] Hellmut von Schweinitz, *Buddhismus und Christentum* (*"Glauben und Wissen,"* Nr. 14 [Munich: Ernst Reinhardt, 1955]), p. 11.

[7] U Hla Bu, "The Christian Encounter with Buddhism in Burma," *IRM*, XLVII (1958), 171.

[8] Edward Conze, *Im Zeichen Buddhas,* trans. Marianne Winder (Frankfurt/M and Hamburg: Fischer-Bücherei, 1957), p. 7. See also *Buddhist Texts Through the Ages,* trans. and ed. Edward Conze *et al.* (New York:

Islam

Islam, too, has been an evangelizing religion since its inception. Its confession of faith, "There is no God but Allah and Mohammed is his prophet," gave its spread an unparalleled dynamic for setting mankind under the theocracy of Allah and including everyone in the Dar-ul-Islam, the "house of Islam." This is not accomplished as long as there are kafirs, i.e., infidels. Mohammed had all of mankind in mind. It is an exaggeration and a distortion, to be sure, but it reproduces the spirit which is present in Islam when the introduction to the Quran states:

No one before the Holy Prophet of Islam ever directed a message to all mankind; no book before the Quran was directed to all mankind. It is the Holy Prophet who says, "Speak, O Mankind, truly, I am a messenger of Allah to all of you." . . . [If the Quran had not been revealed] the world would never have discovered that it has but one creator and it would also never have recognized that its creation serves a great purpose.[9]

God's redemptive will and the Gospel's claim to be the salvation of all mankind are thus completely ignored here. It is surprising that the spread of Islam continued even in periods of

---

Philosophical Library, 1957) p. 7, in which Conze adds that the technical terms "are likely in due course to be absorbed" into English as well.

[9] *Der Heilige Quran: Arabisch-Deutsch,* translated into the German and with an extensive Introduction by Hazrat Mirza Bashiruddin Mahmud Ahmad *et al.* (Zurich and Hamburg: Ahmadiyya-Mission des Islams, 1954), pp. 24–25.

The Ahmadiyya Society has also published an English translation: *The Holy Quran: Arabic Text, Translation and Commentary,* trans. Maulana Muhammad Ali (4th rev. ed.; Lahore, Pakistan: Ahmadiyya Anjuman Ishaat Islam, 1951). We shall use the word Quran to refer to the German edition and particularly to the material in the Introduction, which is quite explicit in its criticism of Christianity and in the claims it makes for Islam. The word Koran will be used for the sacred writings of Islam without this interpretation and commentary.

The English edition, which has a shorter Introduction than the German, gives the material corresponding to the German Introduction only as footnotes. It is extensively indexed, however, for the Ahmadiyya interpretation of the Koran. The English Quran that was first published in 1909—almost fifty years before the Introduction of the German edition—completely lacked the sharply critical attitude toward Christianity and the extreme messianic self-consciousness which characterize the German Introduction. Comparison of the two approaches dramatically demonstrates the change in attitude described by Vicedom during the first half of the twentieth century.

stagnation and political defeats. Alongside this spontaneous spread, Islam has today organized missionary work in the Ahmadiyya sect and other orders, which is based upon the mission-consciousness of the founder: "God promised the chosen Messiah, 'I shall carry your message to the ends of the earth.'"

Today missionary zeal and missionary mandate have come together in the world religions in a growing missionary activity. We have the missionary mandate, but what about our conviction that God's redemption belongs to all men, and what about our missionary zeal?

2. THE MISSION-CONSCIOUSNESS OF THE RELIGIONS

We are confronted today with a resurgence of the religions. One must be aware of their new spirit in order to understand what is going on in the world. There is a change which has overwhelmed us Christians in our introverted and surfeited existence.

The religions of Asia have become aware of their worth. This is evident in the fact that they have broken out of the geographical bounds within which they were hitherto confined. They have themselves carried the battle over to the Christian parts of the world. Asia has begun a world-wide missionary campaign.[10]

Hinduism

It was primarily the Indian, Vivekananda (1862–1902), who as a result of his experiences at the Congress of Religions in Chicago in 1893 brought to the Indians the conviction "that the Hindu faith had within it all the traits of a religion which was intended for all mankind."[11] After him it was Gandhi who gave India a new vision. These and other men have had such an influence that Hinduism has received an awareness of mission. "Indian thought and life have been transformed and her mind

---

[10] Fritz Blanke, "Asiatische religiöse Strömungen in Europa," in *Die Einheit der Kirche und die Sekten* (Zollikon: Evangelischer Verlag, 1957), p. 95.
[11] *Ibid.*, p. 96. See also Devanandan, *op. cit.*, pp. 14 ff. and Kraemer, *World Cultures and World Religions: The Coming Dialogue* (Philadelphia: Westminster Press, 1960), pp. 126 ff.

has been given a new direction."[12] Radhakrishnan himself became India's apostle and gave the people direction. Mankind could be helped only by the Indic spirit of submission to the Divine. Man, turned inward by the Hindu teachings, would become ethical man and thus no longer be a danger to himself. This assertion was proven by the success of Gandhi, who freed India by means of "non-violence" and gave to the Indic people the conviction "that his non-violence was valid for all men and under all circumstances. He wanted to make a universal contribution to the ideal of true humanity."[13]

Buddhism

Even stronger is the awareness of mission in Buddhist territory. During the Jubilee years, in Matara, Ceylon (a place with a large Christian population), a globe with a diameter of three meters was set up. Buddha was enthroned on the globe of the world as priest and world savior. Buddhism, as the light of Asia, now belongs to the whole world. Buddhists hold that the contemporary world, due to the moral collapse of the Christian peoples, is especially receptive to Buddhism, and it is their conviction that only Buddhism can help perplexed humanity. This even leads the English Buddhist Christmas Humphreys to say, "Of all the great religions, Buddhism alone has applied itself to the problem of evil and suffering and solved it."[14] It will therefore also increasingly influence the world. The German monk, Nyanatiloka (Walter Florus Gueth) was of the same conviction: "In summarizing, we can state that instead of having a destructive influence on the people—as is so often asserted in the West—Buddhism, on the contrary, of all religions of the world, is best suited for improving and raising the character and manners of a people."[15] In the same periodical we read: "We are

---

[12] S. Radhakrishnan, *Eastern Religions and Western Thought* (New York: Oxford University Press, 1959), p. 305.
[13] Wolff, *op. cit.*, p. 55.
[14] Humphreys, *op. cit.*, p. 229. See also Kraemer, *op. cit.*, pp. 156 ff.
[15] Nyanatiloka, "Über die Beeinflussung eines Volkes durch den Buddhismus," *Einsicht,* 1956, pp. 58–59.

living in an epoch-making period of transition in the history of Buddhism, such as has perhaps not occurred since the days of the great emperor Asoka."[16] Since under Asoka Buddhism experienced its greatest expansion, this judgment may be somewhat exaggerated. We should, nevertheless, take it seriously.

Islam

While the other religions somehow continue to have the awareness that they are only a part of an "over-all religion," Islam designates itself as *the* religion, as the end result of all revelation, and thereby raises the claim that it is absolute. It wants to unite all men within itself, to overcome or swallow up all other religions. Every Moslem is convinced of this mandate. The Ahmadiyya proclaims that Islam is the most perfect religion. Therefore it will gain the victory over all the other religions. "The sun may leave its course and the stars their appointed places; the earth may cease to turn, yet nothing and no one can now hinder the triumph of Islam and the Holy Prophet."[17] One cannot carry the claim any further. This concurs with a seal of the Bahai sect which bears the motto: "In the world of tomorrow the people will salute one flag."

That reminds me of a placard which I saw in the National Exhibition in Djakarta. The world was hidden in darkness; only Indonesia stood in the light. From it the light streamed out into the rest of the world. Where did it come from?—A holy fire burning in the cupped hands of an Indonesian. Thus Indonesia is the bearer of light for the world. That is missionary spirit.

The missionary spirit is encouraged especially by the Ahmadiyya and by the Mohammedaniyya (which is native to Indonesia). Every newcomer into the Ahmadiyya must take the vow: "I shall always regard it as my primary duty to spread Islam."[18] The goal of Islam is all of humanity. Recently

[16] Winfried Petri, "Zur Geschichte und Gegenwartsbedeutung des Buddhismus," *Einsicht*, 1957, p. 171.   [17] *Der Heilige Quran*, p. 160.
[18] Emanuel Kellerhals, *Der Islam: Seine Geschichte, seine Lehre, sein Wesen* (2d ed.; Basel: Baseler Missionsbuchhandlung, 1956), p. 276. See also Kraemer, *op. cit.*, pp. 99 ff.

Mohammad Tharulla Khan, judge at the World Court in The Hague, also expressed this clearly: Islam views the conversion of Germany and Europe as "a step toward converting all mankind to Islam." We could say in reply, the spread of the world religions is no different from the spread of Christianity. A few members accept the mandate and the remainder support them in a spirit of good will. We nevertheless forget here that the effect of a continuing dispersion of members is stronger than the effect of organized evangelism.

3. THE SMALLNESS OF THE WORLD

As the result of technological development in all fields, we no longer perceive the great size of the world. Distances have shrunk. What occurs in one corner of the world can have global consequences within a short time—is broadcast in a few minutes over the whole earth. No one today can live untouched by world events. The world has become one, even though men are not yet united. Economic and political events force men constantly to think and act within this one world. Where they do not do so tensions arise. Basically there is no longer any isolated area, not even in the realm of world views and religion. Today the flame of an idea can rapidly spread to all mankind. No religion can live shut up within itself, nor can the church. Not only do lasting points of contact arise between the religions, but they also interpenetrate one another. Non-Christian religions have understood this much better than has Christianity. The religions have moved so close to one another today that it is actually dangerous to concern oneself only with the Christian religion.

Even the Western Christian or theologian, no matter of which confession, is no longer in a position to carry on an exclusive monologue. The purely internal demonstration of truth of Christianity stands naive and unarmed before the encircling active movement which has broken forth from the non-Christian religions.[19]

Today the religions have approached one another so closely that

[19] Wolff, *op. cit.*, p. 9.

there are no longer any firm fronts; at most, there are open flanks. This situation can be full of great promise for us Christians, if we learn to understand that the revelation of God is always to be distinguished from the religion of men. The situation is also helpful inasmuch as the church no longer needs to seek out the place to preach: The place is directly in front of our door. The situation becomes, however, a judgment upon Christianity if it does not understand that God has directed it to this world. What an apparatus the church has for maintaining the life of its members from generation to generation! The other religions have only traces of this and yet they succeed in being evangelizing religions. Does not the preservation of their lives lie in the fact that their members are aware of what their religion means to them and therefore pass it on to others?

4. THE GEOGRAPHIC POSITION OF CHRISTIANITY

Christians today make up a third of the world population. Despite the great missionary activity of Christianity, this proportion will not increase, because the non-Christian peoples have a higher excess of births over deaths. To be sure, Christianity still has the reputation of being the world's largest religious organization. That does not mean much, because secularism has not fastened itself on the other religions as it has on Christianity. The number of adherents is not as important as the spontaneous witnessing spirit of a religion. It is the missionary drive, not its "cultural level" and its well-ordered organization, which forces a religion out of isolation. In the other religions we are dealing with large bodies which hardly exhibit any organization, but which nevertheless bind their people to themselves in a manner that Christianity no longer can. Christianity is over-organized and even with the help of the ecumenical movement cannot develop the dynamic which characterizes the other religions today.

Opportunities to come out of isolation the church has had abundantly. If we wish to extract a divine meaning from history, we may see in the much-maligned colonial period the church's great opportunity to break through its fateful encirclement. The world was then ruled by "Christian" political powers. Nevertheless, Christianity carried on missionary activities only to the extent that God actually forced it to do so. It saw no opponent in the non-Christian religions and no mandate among the heathen peoples. The colonial period, which can scarcely be justified so far as its social consequences are concerned, might have been the great opportunity for spreading the Gospel. Since the duty to evangelize was carried out only hesitantly, the isolation of Christianity today, after the close of this period, must become apparent with shocking clarity.

If we overlook the young churches, whose existence we really do not regard lightly—they are indeed the real missionary potential and thereby the sign of promise among the peoples!—Christianity possesses only marginal areas of the world. Its influence diminishes to the degree that the balance of history moves toward Asia, because these peoples were conquered by force, and have not been won over spiritually. Today they seek the prototype behind the Western ideal, and the less the West is able to exemplify the ideal, the more the non-Christian religions acquire influence over contemporary mankind. The isolation becomes more obvious in light of the fact that Christianity has fallen into a superficial "bloc" way of thinking—as if one could equate the Western bloc with "Christian" and the Eastern bloc with "anti-Christian"! Must not the churches in the Eastern bloc prove daily that the church can fulfill its duty under any political system? In addition, the non-Christian religions point out to us daily how unchristian the West has become.

The church must extricate itself completely from this political distinction and understand that the Body of Christ also has members in Communist territories. It is significant that today precisely those religions have undertaken to be missionaries to Christianity which have neither submittted themselves to the world claim of communism nor bound themselves to the system of free democracy. They want to prove themselves deliberately as a third power, which can resist and at the same time penetrate both systems. This is especially true of Islam, which has always had the position of a middle bloc. Since it does not separate politics and religion, its religion will expand as a result of its political success. This position of the other religions is a call to Christianity to take heed. Until now Christianity has not grasped that it loses all credibility through the political bickering of its peoples.

The religious awareness of mission and the political and social ambitions of the other religions have placed Christianity today in a competitive situation which has no parallel in history. Christianity cannot go forth under the same banner. It cannot even work with the same means. It is dependent upon its witness alone. It will be more decisive to the degree that it reflects upon its message and presents it in such a fashion that the peoples hear in it God's answer to their many questions. Competition always means a struggle, a putting forth of effort to the end, a decision. If that is admitted, the contemporary situation is one of the most promising that God has given his Christianity.

2

The Renaissance of the Religions

1. CRITICISM BY CHRISTIANITY

The reawakening of the world religions is the great
fact of our time. Many an earlier judgment about them is con-
sequently being corrected. Presumptuous Western superficiality
assumed that outward domination of other peoples would break
their inner strength. Thus these religions should have fallen apart
under the threat of Western arms and under the influence of
Western civilization and technology. Asiatic thinkers today make
fun of this Western naivete.[1] The reawakening of the religions
proves that the inner strength of a religion breaks forth at the
moment when it is most humiliated, when, according to human
judgment, nothing more can be expected of it.

A renaissance is always released when one religion, seeing
the ideal of another, becomes aware of its own inadequacy
and backwardness. This ideal was provided for all three of the
religions under discussion by the Christian mission and by
Western civilization. Christianity became the ideal for the Indic
peoples, and with it they received a standard for judging their
own religions. Only a very few wanted to realize this ideal by

[1] Kavalam Madhiva Panikkar, *Asia and Western Dominance: A Survey
of the Vasco da Gama Epoch of Asian History 1498–1945* (London: George
Allen & Unwin, 1953), pp. 375–457.

14

giving up their own culture. A renaissance has as a second condition that men seek to reach the ideal while maintaining their heritage. Necessarily this desire became even stronger when they realized that from the ideal came not only stimulation and hope, but also a threat which they could counter only with religious powers. This Western influence therefore drove the Indic peoples to search in their own sources and from them to reform their religions. This is the process which brought about the change in the religions. It also explains why the threat coming from the West had to lead to a reaction against Christianity and against Western civilization. We shall develop these points in detail.

Hinduism

It is important to see that in the development of the religions there is present at the outset an affirmative attitude toward the Christian ideal. The leaders of the religions accepted from Christianity the standards for their action and their judgment and applied them to their own religions. Something similar can be said of the content of religion. The monism of India no longer sufficed; therefore a transformation into theism took place. Christ became a central figure in Indic thought. This becomes most apparent in the syncretistic Brahma Samaj, but can also be observed in the nationalistic Arya Samaj. Both accepted the ideal of Christianity. The first sought to perfect the Indic religion on the basis of the Gospel, the second thought to realize the ideal by means of the heritage of Indic ideas. We must keep these facts securely in mind because today one can often hear that the reawakening of the religions is a result of nationalism and thereby a reaction to the anxiety about life coming from the West. Obviously nationalism would encourage this development, but nationalism is not its cause.

The Brahma Samaj was very critical of the Indic religion, recognized the inferiority of both Indic culture and religion, and in 1850 even abandoned the divinity and divine inspiration of the Veda. It even attacked the holy teachings of the transmigration of souls and of the castes. The leaders sought a faith

with a personal god and a social order modeled according to
Christian ethical principles. This development later turned
against the very Christianity which had given those men the
impetus toward a spiritual renewal of India.

Buddhism

In Buddhism the renaissance set in much later. First the
theosophists, H. S. Olcott and Mme. H. P. Blavatsky, had to
come to Ceylon and arouse Buddhism against Christianity.
Anagarika Dharmapal (1864–1933), a student of Olcott, traveled
over the whole world, made propaganda for Buddhism, and
collected money from Christians for its revitalization! He also
founded the first Buddhist missionary society.[2] Buddhism was
awakened from its Sleeping Beauty nap primarily by Christians.
They were enthusiastic about it and gave it the awareness of
having universal value. Christian countries gave it the financial
means for renewal, for realizing the impulses toward reawakening.

Islam

Islam was the last to participate in the renaissance. When
in the previous century Christian mission and Western civilization challenged the religions, Islam retired immediately into
its shell. Moreover the colonial governments did everything in
order not to stir it up. Many even publicized it as *the* religion
of the colored peoples and contributed to its spread, especially
in Africa. It was the Persian Djamal Al-Din Al-Afghani (d. 1897),
and the Egyptian Muhammad Abduh (d. 1905), who wanted to
adapt Islam to the modern world. The former espoused Pan-Islam-
ism over against the "imperialistic" claims of the West; the latter
sought to adapt the theology of Islam to modern thought.[3]
Renewal succeeded primarily because of rising nationalism, in
which Turkey took the lead. As a result of the Second World
War, most Moslems have received their political freedom, and

[2] S. Kulandran, *Resurgent Religions* ("World Evangelism Today," No. 1
[London: Lutterworth Press, 1957]), p. 16.
[3] Alfred Nielsen, "Can Islam be 'Modern'?," *IRM*, XLIV (1955), 258.

where they are still subject to non-Moslem governments, a bitter struggle for freedom goes on. Since in political victory they always see a superiority of Allah over the enemy, political development gives Islam great stimulus.

Kulandran establishes that in all religions the renaissance had the same causes and led to similar results.[4] It was released by the conflict with Christianity. It was always the result of efforts by definite individuals. It was borne along by the wish for political freedom. It was completed by the rebirth of native culture and language. The results can be summarized thus: Each religion has converted itself into a modern religion and today raises claim to being able to solve all mankind's problems. In each religion the missionary spirit has developed until today the claim to universal validity is raised. We could also point to a sense of optimism and a superiority, not unlike that of the West, but we should not overlook the fact *that* these religions let themselves be called to renewal, even though the genuineness of the motives can be doubted.

2. THE INFLUENCE OF THE NEW IDEAL

Unquestionably the ideal which came from Western civilization made a strong impression on the members of the other religions. This ideal was provided primarily by the colonial powers. Since the non-Christians regard the social position of a man as the result of his religion, the outward superiority of Western man—his different way of life, his technological equipment and especially his scientific advance — were naturally ascribed to the religion of the West, Christianity. Among the non-Christian peoples this first of all necessarily released a feeling of inferiority, which among the Buddhist and Islamic peoples expressed itself in the gloomy feeling that their peoples were bound by fate to a subordinate position. They therefore sought salvation in the affirmation of their tradition and wanted

---

[4] Kulandran, *op. cit.*, pp. 5 ff. See also P.D. Devanandan, *The Shock of the Discovery of World Religions*, in History's Lessons for Tomorrow's Mission (Geneva: WSCF, 1960), pp. 216 ff.

to rescue their existence and way of life by means of this protection against Western civilization. They did not succeed in this, however. A Buddhist university professor recently wrote: "Under foreign domination Buddha's Sasana, like the waning moon, has been disappearing gradually."[5] Because this traditional position set up great obstacles, both religions were evangelized only negligently by Christianity, so that eventually only the disturbing ideal of Western civilization was transmitted to them, which forthwith put them to sleep.

Hinduism

The situation was otherwise in India, where Christian missionary work was initiated energetically and, through the preaching of the Gospel and through Christian good works, offered a religiously based and ethically determined ideal of human life. This ideal worked in such a way through the person of Jesus that in the course of time Jesus became for the Indic peoples the ideal of Indic perfection. According to this ideal the other religions were judged, ethical standards were established, and the spirit of surrender was demanded. An approach to Christianity therefore followed. One sought to make Hinduism more like Christianity. This development was greeted by the Christian missions as very promising, but basically it only served to modernize Hinduism and to realize the ideal. The Brahma Samaj, founded by Ram Mohan Roy, an organization of deeply spiritual thinkers which was never very large, but which exercised a deep influence upon the Indian people, became the carrier of this movement in India.

Ram Mohan Roy (1774–1833) was first moved to reform Hinduism through contact with the monotheism of Islam. He studied all the religions of India, but turned to Christianity and even learned the original biblical languages. Thereby, however, he also came into contact with the Enlightenment in Europe. He wanted to cleanse popular Hinduism of its superstitions and

[5] Addison J. Eastman, "The Sixth Buddhist Council," *IRM*, XLIII (1954), 282.

restore the religion in its original form again. In the Vedas and the Upanishads he thought to detect a certain monotheism. For him Jesus was the fulfiller of Hinduism, a great moralist, who in the Sermon on the Mount had announced the norms of the relationship to God and of ethical conduct. "His position is that Christ was a theist like himself, that His disciples had misunderstood Him, and that the whole edifice of Christology is a huge mistake."[6] His book, *The Precepts of Jesus, the Guide to Peace and Happiness*, interprets the Gospel in this spirit. It "is a reply to the missionaries rather than a call to Indians."[7]

For Ram Mohan Roy, Jesus was only a figure who should give a new understanding to Hinduism. In order to spread this he founded the above-mentioned society, which is a theistic organization or movement. This organization should lead the Hindus back to a monotheistic faith. The really great followers of Ram Mohan Roy have remained true to this goal. Debendra Nath Tagore and Keshab Chandra Sen have deepened his teachings. Christ was more and more assimilated into Indic thought. They were supported by their followers in this concern. All regarded Jesus as only a great teacher among other teachers, who could be used for Hinduism.[8] Christianity thus gave the model and Jesus the ideal. Hindus accepted both, not in order to convert themselves to the Christian faith, but in order to make Hinduism into an attractive religion. The Gospel was rendered harmless through absorption and assimilation.

Buddhism

I know of no similar attempt in Buddhism. The Buddhists speak of Jesus with great respect, but they see in him only a great teacher of mankind. For them he can be nothing other than an incarnation of the Buddha-principle. Since Jesus cannot be understood at all without his belief in God, and the Buddhists

[6] I. N. Farquhar, *Modern Religious Movements in India* (New York: The Macmillan Company, 1924), p. 32.
[7] Panikkar, *op. cit.*, p. 321.
[8] Otto Wolff, *Indiens Beitrag zum neuen Menschenbild: Ramakrishna, Gandhi, Sri Aurobindo* (Hamburg: Rowohlt, 1957), p. 13.

theoretically do not believe in a god, they can use Jesus only as a moral example. In contrast it is worth noting that Western intellectuals seek a synthesis between Buddha and Jesus. A significant attempt is the work of von Schweinitz, in which the dependence of Jesus upon Buddha is indeed left open, but the possibility is given foundation.[9]

Buddhism opened itself to Western influence much later than Hinduism, and only under the pressure of necessity. Where Western civilization has penetrated up to now in the interior of India and in southeast Asia, its influence has had no great significance because, so it seems, those peoples are not impressed by the things of this world. Hence religion has not yet led to any attempt to free them from the conditions of their existence and thereby free them from their external suffering. With the exception of Ceylon, southern Buddhism takes the stand that all progress must grow out of religion! In this way it cannot harm the people! Therefore it is a great concern of the President of Burma, U Nu, to awaken Buddhism. He has actually managed to use Buddhism to solve many problems in post-war Burma. Where, however, progress is to grow out of religion, it will be unavoidable that the religion involved modify its goals. The modernization of Buddhist monasticism which has made the monks a sort of spiritual police force is the best proof of this.

The problem of the renewal of Buddhism lies less in its opposition to Christianity than in its tie to the Indic motherland. This has undergone the greatest religious change. From the slumbering godhead has emerged a world-shaping deity. Will Buddhism be able to do without this religious drive in the building up of its states? Already today it is becoming evident that through emphasis on the Buddha-principle it is falling back into the belief in the Brahman. The more it seeks to win India back, the more it will fall victim to the great amalgamating process of Hinduism. The reformation of Hinduism will therefore become a question of existence for Buddhism.

[9] Hellmut von Schweinitz, *Buddhismus und Christentum* (*"Glauben und Wissen,"* Nr. 14 [Munich: Ernst Reinhardt, 1955]), pp. 53–57.

Islam

Things are different in Islam. The ideal of Christianity has scarcely made an impression here, which does not mean that individual Moslems have not been attracted—especially by the practice of Christian love. The Islamic peoples did not accept any religious impetus from Christianity. In contrast they were most strongly attracted by Western civilization. Due to its pomp-loving princes, even Saudi-Arabia, which espouses the puritanical teachings of the Wahabi sect, cannot shut itself away from the influence of technology and civilization. Hence, for example, the pilgrimage industry in Mecca has been completely modernized. In Islam the primary issue has been to find the synthesis between the Koran and Western technology, industry, and science. Many Mohammedan intellectuals attempt to prove that the whole progressive development is already foreshadowed in the Koran.

This point of view is held most strongly in the Ahmadiyya sect, where every religion is actually explained in a rationalistic, if not Marxistic, fashion as the result of a stage in the development of mankind. To this is added the evidence that Islam as the youngest religion most closely corresponds to the present development of mankind. The Quran edited by the Ahmadiyya also points out that the building of the Suez and Panama Canals was predicted in the Koran. On the other hand, 172 pages are used to show what an obscure book the Bible is, which can in no way stand up against science.[10] Naturally only those parts in it are true which can be referred to Mohammed. While Jesus is still always treated with respect in the Koran, in this Quran he is presented as the great teacher of error. Here then Jesus is not the model, but must serve to show the superiority of Mohammed.

As a result of our study we can say that Christianity served to restore and modify each religion. How much these religions have taken over in detail from Christianity in this process must now be established.

---

[10] *Der Heilige Quran: Arabisch-Deutsch*, translated and with an extensive introduction by Hazrat Mirza Bashiruddin Mahmud Ahmad *et al.* (Zurich and Hamburg: Ahmadiyya-Mission des Islams, 1954), pp. 25 ff. and 122.

3. PURIFICATION OF THE RELIGIONS

Hinduism

Here again we shall begin with Hinduism because the process is most clearly delineated in it. Jesus as the example served at the same time as a critic of the religions, a process in which, to be sure, the question was never raised concerning the extent to which the social message was contained in the New Testament itself. The ideal was accepted as it was represented by the mission. Panikkar says of the Brahma Samaj:

> Its social message was Westernization, to purge Hinduism of the customs and superstitions with which it was overlaid, to raise the status of women, to bridge the gulf between popular and higher Hinduism, to fight relentlessly against caste, social taboo, polygamy, and other well-entrenched abuses. To the educated Hindu, who felt unsettled in mind by the attack of the missionaries, the Brahmo Samaj provided the way out.[11]

Similarly war was declared on polytheism. Many of these proposals aroused great opposition among orthodox Hindus. However, since Ram Mohan Roy and his followers attacked the abuses more and more and caused the government to set them aside, the reforms steadily gained ground. Thus already in 1828 suttee could be forbidden. Strongest and most enduring was the caste system, which was legally forbidden only by free India, without being forced out of existence in practice. Progress against child marriage could be made only after the First World War, when the age of marriage was set at fourteen years. With this reform began a rapid growth of the school system. The more Indians studied, the more the country became open to social reforms.

Buddhism

In the Buddhist territory, people had always had a higher morality, hence the reforms did not appear in this fashion. Although in Ceylon and Burma, Buddhism was separated from the state, it remained such a power that the educated had to identify them-

---

[11] Panikkar, *op. cit.*, p. 321.

selves with it if they wished to achieve a position through the colonial government. Only as Buddhists did they have influence over the people. In Siam reforms were hardly possible. Since Buddhism trains its people to deny the world, so-called progress can make no great impression on the people. Today, however, these people are also tending toward a Western orientation.

Islam

In Islam the Ahmadiyya, especially, criticized tradition. Islam did bring about unified thinking among several peoples, but the Arabic culture did not spread in equal measure with Islam's expansion. Since each people retained its own culture, a modernization could only be undertaken locally. Most advanced of the Moslem countries today is Turkey, which introduced a modern system of law, raised the position of women, brought the schools to a high standard, banished harems, and gave life a modern appearance.

4. THE PERFECTING OF THE RELIGIONS

These reforms would not have been possible if the leaders of the religions had not tried to give their people new religious thoughts and impulses. Since their own resources did not suffice, they borrowed from Christianity. Thus a syncretistic process was introduced which even today has not been terminated. It shows to a startling degree, for instance, how for nationalistic reasons India raises claims to Jesus without binding itself to the fundamentals of his revelation. Since in the opinion of the Indic people religions are common property, they are naturally then at everyone's disposal. Thus the Gospel was used to supplement Hinduism. Without question that was the strongest means of neutralizing the Christian mission.

Hinduism

If we ignore the influences of civilization here, it was primarily the Christian revelation which had the greatest influence upon Ram Mohan Roy and his followers, but always, however, only to

the extent that it confirmed the theism found in the Vedas. Only
that which did not contradict Hinduism was accepted. The result
was, of course, that much Christian material was misinterpreted.
Among the leaders of the Brahma Samaj it was Keshab Chandra
Sen (1838–84) who especially recognized the significance of
the person of Jesus. From him came the familiar words: "Only
one deserves the heart of India, and this one shall have it—Jesus
Christ." For a long time he lived in a Christ-mysticism.

Wolff describes the development in this way: Under Ram
Mohan Roy, Jesus became the ethical leader, under Keshab
Chandra Sen the universal atoner, under Gandhi the prince of
peace.[12] Perhaps we can best make the development clear to our-
selves if we repeat the statements of faith of the Brahma Samaj.
I cite them in shortened form according to Chantapie de la
Saussaye. The complete form is in Farquhar. Debendra Nath
Tagore (1817–1905) formulated the following statements: (1)
God is a person with high moral qualities. (2) God is never incarnate. (3) God hears and grants our prayers. (4) God must
be worshiped only in spirit. The Hindu asceticism, temple forms,
and cult forms are not required. All castes and races can reach
God through their worship. (5) Repentance and ceasing to sin
are the only means which lead to forgiveness and salvation.
(6) God reveals himself directly in nature. No book is binding.

In 1878, a splinter group of the Brahma Samaj added the following new articles: (7) God is the father of all men and all are
brothers. (8) The soul is immortal and its development is
eternal. (9) God rewards the good and punishes the sinner,
but his punishment does not last forever. Keshab formulated his
own statements in addition: (10) God is a trinity—father, son,
and spirit—and as father he is simultaneously the great mother.
(11) The teaching of Brahma is no new religion, but the heart
of all religions. It is God's lost directive and its missionaries are
God's chosen apostles. (12) We learn to know God in nature and

[12] Wolff, "Wandlung des Christusbildes im modernen Hinduismus,"
Evangelische Missions-Zeitschrift (hereafter referred to as *EMZ*), 1956, pp.
pp. 65 ff.

by indirect observation, but he reveals himself also in inspired men and proclaims his will to them, giving direct commands to his servants.[13]

We recognize in these sentences how these men have struggled with the problem of a personal god, and how the God of the Bible in Jesus Christ remained a mystery to them. The further this development progressed, the more the Christian revelation was trapped in these statements, weakened and given a Hinduistic interpretation. Thus the way is cleared for an Indic mysticism. Everything has to serve to strengthen Hinduism. It is the mother of all religion and now becomes missionary religion.

Keshab went so far as to found the Church of the New Dispensation. He believed that God revealed himself today just as in earlier times and also that he himself was a bearer of revelation. To begin with he placed all founders of religion on one plane. Gradually he grew into a Christ-mysticism, but without recognizing the uniqueness of Jesus. His church also seeks, however, "a synthesis with the characteristic Hindu piety of the centuries."[14]

In the same period these men were joined by the great religious philosophers of India who gave Hinduism new direction and missionary impulse: Ramakrishna, Vivekananda, and Aurobindo. They were either mystics or ascetic philosophers who made Hinduism attractive to all men. Looking back, Wolff felt able to say that there could hardly be an important Indian "who does not explicitly recognize the positive enrichment, development and revolution which Christianity has brought to the total Indic life."[15]

As part of this perfecting of the religions, India, upon the basis of the new ethical principles and the newly acquired ideal of man, and following the example of the missions, itself decisively took in hand the solution of human needs. The Rama-

[13] Chantepie de la Saussaye, *Lehrbuch der Religionsgeschichte,* ed. Alfred Bertholet, Edvard Lehmann, *et al.* (4th ed.; Tübingen: J. C. B. Mohr, 1925), II, 65 ff. The complete form of these statements is given by Farquhar, *op. cit.,* pp. 71 ff.
[14] Wolff, *Indiens Beitrag . . . ,* p. 45.   [15] *Ibid.,* p. 136.

krishna Mission, an organization founded by Vivekananda, established approximately a hundred centers in India for benevolent activities according to a definite program: encouragement of learning; preparation of teachers, doctors, and professors; educational work among the masses; establishment of a large school system up to the university level; technical workshops; institutions of mercy; printing and publishing houses; and agricultural reforms and work in the villages. Sivananda founded similar institutions through his "Divine Life Society." His broad social program was intended to help the Indic peoples to join the modern family of man. This practical activity was especially connected with the Ashrams. The greatest project, probably, took place in Pondicherry, taking in a fourth of the city and numbering more than three hundred houses.[16] In free India, Vinobaji founded the Bhoodan, i.e., the movement for land distribution, and through its activity he has stimulated land reform to benefit the landless through the proclamation of the love of neighbor. During his meetings he also holds worship services not unlike the Christian. At such a service he spoke the following bidding prayer: "Lift up your hearts to God. Come before Him and let Him fill you with His peace! Let him make His Spirit yours! Think of a person and pray for him—Pray that your prayer may touch him."[17] He is celebrated today as the great messiah of India. Here Hinduism presents itself as the great imitator of Christianity.

We can sum up what has been said with a word from the Indian, David G. Moses: "Hinduism has taken an enormous amount of the content of the Christian Faith into its own. Not that it has openly acknowledged its debt. On the contrary: every reinterpretation of Hindu doctrine has been introduced as a rediscovery of what was already there. Only one thing it has not been able to do—to absorb Jesus Christ."[18]

[16] Ibid., pp. 17, 108.
[17] Blaise Levai, "India on the March," IRM, XLVI (1957), 195.
[18] David G. Moses, "Christianity and the Non-Christian Religions," IRM, XLIII (1954), 153.

Buddhism

The same thing cannot be said in the area of Buddhism, except for northern Buddhism which has often copied the Christian church even in the smallest details. Since Buddhism has only lately been open to the influence of the West, it has adopted little that is Western. Buddhism today is much more fascinated by the successes of Hinduism than by Christianity! It has again taken up the belief in the supernatural, permits the worship of gods, and takes a positive attitude toward the things of the world, especially in areas where the Buddhist peoples have achieved political freedom. Thus Buddhism has again found a national task. In this connection, it certainly must not be overlooked that today its ethical ideals coincide in large measure with those of the Gospel. Nirvana is often described today in Christian terms. In addition, the spirit of self-sacrifice in the service of others is encouraged. Many philanthropic undertakings go back to the influence of Christianity.[19]

Islam

Nor is there much to be said about Islam. Since it conceives itself to be the perfect religion and thus the realization of all religion, and it claims to have the best social order, its feeling of superiority has made it immune to Christian influence. Whoever reads the introduction to the Quran can recognize how all ethical ideals which Jesus brought to mankind are either designated as less valuable or are ascribed to Mohammed. He is the great prophet with whom the new age begins.[20]

In all this it becomes clear that the religions have picked much fruit from the tree of Christianity; however, they have not accepted Christ, but have left him behind. That is also true where, as in India, the crucifix is found in the homes and the temples, and even where the Christian worship service is imitated and the people pray to Jesus. He is not the Savior, but only a guide for mankind's self-centered thinking about redemption. Thus

[19] U Hla Bu, "The Christian Encounter with Buddhism in Burma," *IRM*, XLVII (1958), 176.   [20] *Der Heilige Quran*, p. 22.

those religions leave Christ behind. They live by him and yet at the same time they close themselves to his message! Their development is unthinkable without Christ, but they have made themselves immune to Christ.[21]

5. THE RELIGIONS FIND THEMSELVES

After a long crisis the religions have found themselves. Their revival began when their self-confidence was shaken. The representatives of the religions recognized very early, either through their studies in the West or through contact with the representatives of Christianity in their own lands, that one can have the results of the Christian faith without having to take over the Christian doctrine. This astonishing discovery drove them to seek more and more zealously in their own sources to find a synthesis between their own culture and the new ideals. The next discovery was, for example, that they could thus remain completely Indians. Therefore they did not need to break with their heritage. One could take up this new thing for oneself without arousing opposition from the Christians. In addition they were instructed in the value of their own religion by the representatives of Western history of religions. That gave them courage for self-determination and self-realization.

Hinduism

Ramakrishna and Vivekananda, with their deep mysticism, decisively influenced this self-discovery. Brahma, which up until now had been thought of as resting within itself, they made the active and creative subject of all activity, and the world of appearance they made the arena of divine activity. Thus they changed the unworldly attitude of Hinduism into a world-oriented attitude, without at the same time placing man with his egotistic and selfish will in the foreground. Brahma is all, while man is only a hull in and through which the divine works. Ramakrishna could go so far here that even in the sex act he

---

[21] W. Freytag, "Der Islam als Beispiel einer nachchristlichen Religion," *EMZ*, 1955, p. 2.

saw the divine at work. "God is always in everything, in pleasure as in pain, in victory as in decay, in friend as in foe."[22] This teaching admits of no resistance. Man can only surrender himself to the divine and let the divine work in him. Brahma is always the good which makes the world better. That such a doctrine is nothing but a deepened fatalism was not seen. Through Vivekananda it was, moreover, made into a message for the world.

Ramakrishna did not want to abolish human nature with this mysticism. He knew that man can resist the divine. He believed, however, that the divine takes up a place in man and becomes the motive power of his actions. In this Ramakrishna broke with the "All-is-One" mysticism according to which man must enter the divine. He pointed out the opposite road to salvation. According to it, man must only be at the disposal of the divine. Through the divine man realizes a duty to himself and to the world. Thus he receives a divine directive.

After them, Mahatma Gandhi next made Indic teaching bear fruit for the freeing of his people. Wolff points out that Gandhi in his fight for freedom could not do much with Ramakrishna's submission to the divine, nor with the teachings of Jesus.[23] They served him personally for spiritual orientation. Gandhi, however, was a dichotomous or antinomian person, for whom truth and the freedom of India stood higher than submission to God. Thus Gandhi's teaching of non-violence is different from Ramakrishna's. For him non-violence can also be a sharp instrument of force whenever it is necessary for India's sake. In one respect Gandhi's position is clearer than Ramakrishna's, however; he acts directly from the basis of established Hinduism and himself contributes much to making it stronger. It dictates to him the maxims of his action and the goal of his contribution. Gandhi actually makes Hinduism a world religion. He gives it a sense of purpose which lets all searching retreat into the background.

[22] Wolff, op. cit., p. 16.
[23] Wolff, Mahatma und Christus: Eine Charakterstudie Mahatma Gandhis und des modernen Hinduismus (Berlin: Lettner Verlag, 1955), pp. 11–12.

His teaching is a great religious political program. Gandhi gives Hinduism great practical tasks through which this religion finds itself.

Buddhism

Since the eighth century Buddhism has not developed much activity outside its own realm. At that time it began to be absorbed by Hinduism and to be driven out of India. Since then Buddhism has rested within itself and fallen prey, as von Schweinitz shows, to "inner hollowness and emptiness of mind."[24] Southern Buddhism brought forth no reformation, while in northern Buddhism there was always present a certain conflict among the various sects over doctrine and the correct way of life. There Buddhism also found a new cultural task. The history of Japan and China is often determined by the influence of Buddhism or the reaction against it. In the south, on the other hand, Buddhism slumbered within itself. It was satisfied (according to Kulandran) when Buddha was honored by the people, when the kings cared for Buddhism as its protectors, when the dharma, i.e., the Buddhist rules for living, were followed, and when the monastic order (sangha) had a preferred place among the people.[25] The sangha deeply influenced the people. Of necessity it lost its significance, however, to the degree that the lives of the people were determined by the colonial government. Therefore the assault of nationalism aroused the powers in Buddhism. Buddhism did not first have to find itself because it had not been lost to the West. It has not made itself conform to the contemporary situation, but has sought to master the situation through its doctrine. Because the modern situation has challenged it, its awareness of mission has reawakened.

It was above all U Nu who set Buddhism a new task. "He has espoused the cause of Buddhism with energy, enthusiasm, determination and imagination . . . He appeals to the modern practical man to test for himself the claim of Buddhism that

[24] von Schweinitz, *op. cit.*, p. 22.
[25] Kulandran, *op. cit.*, p. 17.

it alone can bring peace of mind and freedom from desires."[26]
Everything will now depend upon how widely the results of
the Council of Rangoon are utilized. There Buddhist intellectuals
armed themselves for the encounter with the contemporary world.

Islam

In Islam in the eighteenth century there arose the reform
movement of the Wahabi sect, which was limited, to be sure, to
the Arab regions, and which sought the salvation of Islam in a
return to the original sources. Its members wanted to cleanse
Islam of alien traits. It was a puritanical movement which strongly emphasized the laws of Allah. It still has great influence in
North Africa. Kulandran tells us that we can expect no renaissance in Islam, for belief in the letter of the law so limits life
that every innovation is regarded as a sin against Allah. No
change in doctrine, such as is apparent in Hinduism, is possible.
Every criticism would be an offense against the divinity of the
prophet, against the Koran and against Allah. The Ahmadiyya
permits itself to do much criticizing. It dare do this, however,
only because it is the one that wants to give the Koran universal
meaning. At the same time, in contrast to Hinduism and
Buddhism, it addresses itself to human greed and claims that
only Mohammed brought glory, wealth, and polygamy to mankind. In this it counts too heavily on men's ignorance. Modern
Moslem lands prove the contrary. Moslem glory and wealth
always supported itself upon conquests. Now that the Moslems
have no Christians or "heathen" to pay tribute, there is no longer
much wealth in evidence.

The process of self-discovery is not finished. Even today all
religions are still being challenged by the increasing influence
of civilization, technology, and industrialization. The people who
are involved feel that they are losing their culture in the face
of these changes and that their social security is being destroyed.
That gives all religions a new stimulus. Since Christianity itself
is felt to be a factor in this development, they expect no help

[26] U Hla Bu, op. cit., p. 173.

from it. An attempt is made along religious lines to find the synthesis of the contemporary situation with true humanity. That is now the case even in Africa, where many believe they can rescue their own culture only if they return to their old religion. In Asia this concern has already become a national program.

6. NATIONALISM

Nationalism among the younger nations is a fairly new occurrence. Usually it is dated from 1905 when Russia, the great European power, was defeated by Japan. This act gave the hope of freedom to all the peoples of Asia. The impetus was already equally strong when in 1893 the Asian representatives to the World Congress of Religions in Chicago recognized that their religions were not inferior to Christianity. Thus Asian nationalism is also religiously determined. The religious nationalism was actually present before the political. It remained confined, however, to small circles. Only when through the First World War the crimes of the white race became fully apparent, when the white race lost all prestige in Asia, did political ambitions become stronger than religious ambitions.

It is significant for this nationalism that it did not free itself from religion. Religion and politics have so influenced each other that it is hard to say which gives the stronger stimulus. In any case, the religions have received strong impetus from nationalism and on the other hand nationalism today still has its basic support in the religions. It is openly "anti-white" and at the same time "anti-Christian." It has not yet thrown up any boundaries among the peoples of Asia. We must emphasize this "not yet," for even the nationalism of Asia will not escape the fate of the separation of the peoples.

Hinduism

The reaction against Western influence arose from the same causes as the assimilation and perfecting. It was an Indian by the name of Mul Sankar, known through the name he assumed

in his order, Dayananda Sarasvati (1824–83), who started a
religious counter-movement against Christianity. Brought up
very strictly by his father, even in youth he had doubts whether
the deity is really only one universal power and whether the
soul is a part of it. He believed rather that God is a person and
that the soul must be separate from him. The world, therefore,
is not appearance, but reality.[27] Under different masters he
sought to deepen this teaching by means of Yoga. He believed
he found his conviction supported in the Vedas and believed
he had to reconstitute Indic religion and culture in its purity.
Only in 1872 after meeting Keshab, and later under the influence of the Theosophical Society, did he develop into a na-
tionalist. In 1875 he founded the Arya Samaj. Through this
organization he transmitted to the Indian people hatred against
everything Christian and Western. His battle cry was: Back to
the Vedas, back to India! "His program included reform for
indigenous religion and extirpation for foreign religion."[28]
Change and progress, he felt, should come from the strength
of the native religion.

The confession of faith of the Arya Samaj can be summed up
in the following sentences: (1) There is only one God. He alone
may be prayed to. He can be worshiped only in spirit and not
through idols. (2) Mankind should be active in righteousness
and men should work together to improve the conditions of life.
(3) The four Vedas contain the knowledge about God. In them
religious truth is given, and all knowledge is hidden in them.
They are given by God out of eternity. Nothing in them is subject
to time or place.

With these statements the Arya Samaj gives its program for
India and asserts Hinduism's claim to absolute validity. All knowledge and all religious truth is contained in the "transcendental
and heavenly knowledge" of the Vedas. Dayananda also referred
all Indian culture to these statements, calling for a return to
the beginnings. Against the Christian teaching of salvation he

[27] Farquhar, *op. cit.*, p. 106.   [28] *Ibid.*, p. 112.

advanced the following statements: The Vedas teach the trans-migration of the soul and karma. Forgiveness is impossible. Salvation is liberation from transmigration of the soul.

Even the Arya Samaj did not have many members. But it espoused the fight against Western influences. Its program was to become very significant for India's nationalism. Without doubt, the decisive person in this was Mahatma Gandhi. He took up the fight for freedom and through his religious attitude helped re-orient the Indian spirit. According to Kulandran, he brought nothing new, but he took over the religious heritage of the Bhagavad-Gita and emphasized some teachings more strongly than the other Indians.[29] We are not interested here in how Gandhi pursued his fight for freedom. We must observe, how-ever, that Gandhi made the doctrine of non-violence the basis of the revolution and carried on the struggle in all its stages with religious means. Thus he showed his compatriots how their re-ligion was suited to great tasks. Hinduism does not render the individual helpless. Non-violence presupposes a greater moral power than does the use of force. Because of his political theory, the movement had to turn against Christianity, which since Con-stantine the Great had accustomed itself "to sanction violence."[30] Gandhi permitted force, however, when it was a matter of India's welfare. Thus national interests stood above religious interests even for him. While Ramakrishna still explained all religions were equally justified because they represented the same truth, Gandhi raised the principle: All religions are equal and are equally true. Therefore one religion must respect the other, and none has the right to carry on missionary activity against another. "It was im-possible for me to regard Christianity as a perfect religion or as the greatest of all religions."[31] Not only is Christian missionary activity in India superfluous, but conversion becomes "the dead-liest poison that ever disturbed the fountain of truth."[32]

---

[29] Kulandran, op. cit., p. 8.   [30] Wolff, Indiens Beitrag . . . , p. 54.
[31] Wolff, Mahatma und Christus . . . , p. 131. Cf. Gandhi's Autobiogra-phy: The Story of My Experiment with Truth, trans. Mahadev Desai (Wash-ington, D.C.: Public Affairs Press, 1948), p. 171.
[32] Wolff, Indiens Beitrag . . . , p. 88.

From here it is only a short step to making Hinduism the *one* religion. Kulandran tells us, as long as the concepts of Brahma and Maya had validity, every religion had justification for its existence. Now, on the other hand, when the good of India took first place, one discovered that the adherents of the other religions in India had fallen away from Hinduism. Now the principle was established that an Indian could only be a Hindu. Now Hinduism claimed the adherents of the other religions and became intolerant. It declared itself the national religion, and whoever doubted this claim became its opponent. "Hinduism wants to enter the field with a stirring battle-cry, warning all antagonists that Hinduism is right and that any denial of this truth means mortal combat."[33] The Mahasabha (the right wing of Hinduism) "united with Brahma Samaj, which D. S. Sarma described as 'the militant ecclesia in the lap of Hinduism,' has as its goal a 100 per cent Hindu India. It is active in seeking to reconvert to Hinduism both Muslims and Christians. It is the main driving force behind all the current efforts to create prejudice against Christians in India and in particular against foreign missionaries."[34]

In this controversy, Christianity is disparaged as the religion of the West. Its value is judged by the behavior of the Western powers. Because the European peoples have shown themselves to be dangerous for Asia, Christianity is marked as a harmful religion. This is the cause of the difficult position of our younger churches in India. Religious freedom is guaranteed by the Indian constitution, yet going over to Christianity is regarded as desertion. Individual conversions are still countenanced; group conversions are no longer to occur. The Mahasabha Party seeks to prevent any missionary activity. It has even proposed a law according to which conversion should be made subject to approval by the police. The Suddhi movement which arose out of this party seeks to bring all Moslems and Christians back to Hinduism. It is significant that Gandhi supported these recon-

[33] Kulandran, *op. cit.*, pp. 11 ff.
[34] Max Warren, *CMS News-Letter*, No. 188, p. 3.

versions to Hinduism, even when they involved large groups, although he sought to prevent mass movements toward Christianity.[35] Through the activity of the Mahasabha, our worship services in India today are disturbed and life is made difficult for the Christians. They are socially at a disadvantage and do not always receive support in the same measure as their non-Christian social equals. In a few cases it has even happened that a Christian church or institution has been burned down. Often Christians are oppressed by mobs. The Indian authorities do not desire this, but cannot do much about it.

Buddhism

The situation is not much different in the Buddhist areas of Ceylon and Burma, where the religion of unending good and compassion for men is said to reign. Ceylon had achieved limited political freedom by 1931. That was the signal to Buddhism to begin political activity. Since then the monks have been seeking to spread dharma among the non-Buddhists, i.e., to convert Hindus and Christians to Buddhism. Thus Buddhism shall also become a national religion. Since 1947, the date of Ceylon's complete independence, it becomes ever clearer that the monks desire to determine life in the state. The Christian church is allowed scarcely any influence in public life. Great difficulties are made in the realm of education. In Burma, too, there is an attempt to motivate Christians to give up their faith. In both countries the monks exercise a sort of spiritual police power over faith and life and are the driving force in the spread of Buddhism. In these countries the kings were always patrons of religion. Because of this the governments, religiously neutral in themselves, are today forced to assume at least a benevolent position toward the activity of the monks. In addition there is the "nationalistic feeling." At the Mission Conference in Ghana, the Secretary for East Asia of the International Missionary Council said: "The reawakening of Buddhism is connected with the

[35] Charles W. Forman, "Freedom of Conversion in India," *IRM*, XLV (1956), 183–184.

achievement of freedom. Today it is ashamed that it has slept for four hundred years under colonial rule. The feeling of freedom gives it a new outlook." In another report of this conference it is stated: "It is completely natural that the first desire of men when they have become free is the wish to determine their own lives. They look back into the past and discover something of their lost grandeur." The religions thus want to make their past alive again and useful for the present.

Islam

Nationalism has a fanatical character in many Moslem countries, especially where the *corpus islamicus* is still threatened by colonial rule. Here, however, nationalism has still another trait; it wants to overcome the great backwardness of the peoples. Since in Islam religion and politics are closely intertwined, modernization of the countries is bound to a religious awakening. Every success is felt to be a sanction on the part of Allah. An attack upon any Moslem country is therefore regarded as being directed against all Islam. It is a basic principle that Moslems shall not be ruled by those of other faiths. We know how this arrangement has worked out in North Africa. For this reason there is a battle for unity in Indonesia, because through partitioning, parts of Moslem populations would come under non-Moslem rule. In all Moslem countries there is forced reconversion; in many there is even persecution of Christians.

The changed religions thus want to assert themselves at any cost. Since religious and national communities coincide, these religions must become political and can therefore also understand Christianity only as a political religion. Hence these men turn against the Christian church on political grounds. The church is today a great irritation among these peoples, because it encloses its faithful in a separate community.

7. THE ABSOLUTE CHARACTER OF THE RELIGIONS' CLAIM

The present antagonism toward Christianity cannot be correctly evaluated if we make nationalism alone responsible for it.

By the change that has taken place, the religions feel themselves justified in questioning Christianity's claim to be absolute. Islam has always done that and has designated itself as the only rightful religion. Hence today fronts are thrown up which never existed before. Significantly, the controversy does not result from the world religions' allowing the Gospel to put the question of truth to them, but precisely in that the substantial equality, and thereby the equal justification of all religions, is emphasized. If the religions are variants of a great whole and different ways to the one truth, then naturally each religion has the right to offer itself as a help to mankind. Unfortunately we in Christianity have not yet noticed that with this attitude the vital nerve of our faith is disturbed. Today we are the ones being questioned by these religions. What is at stake is not merely the philosophical concept of the claim of absolutism, but the message of the Gospel: the message of salvation through Jesus Christ.

The religions today, to be sure, still recognize one another but on the other hand they have taken up missionary activity against one another and thereby place each other in question. Thus Hinduism today conceives of Buddhism as only a part of itself and lays claim to the Buddhist peoples. Buddhism, however, would like to win back India. Hinduism carries on mission work in India against Islam and against Christianity. Islam, however, tries to win the Hindus in Pakistan. That is an indication of what may come. All three religions are agreed that Christianity must be eliminated from their own territories. It is thus not recognized that Christianity is an Asiatic religion which set foot in India at the same time that it pressed forward toward the West. Because today the foreign religions live upon opposition to the West, they have therefore begun a spiritual conflict with Christianity. It must, however, be said for Buddhism that until now it has launched from Asia no significant efforts in the controversy. Instead many Western representatives of Buddhism are stepping into the conflict, however. They believe they can demonstrate not only the derivative character of Christianity, but also the moral and redemptive superiority of Buddhism.

Hinduism

In the conflict one detects the change which the religions have undergone. If until Ramakrishna it was still true that Christianity provided the model for reform, there has since been an attempt to indicate Hinduism as the model and to derive Christianity from it. Gandhi could say, "My religion is Hinduism, which for me is the religion of mankind and includes the best of all religions known to me."[36] The New Testament is for Gandhi only an affirmation of his basic Indic ideas; only to this extent does he recognize it. Even the Sermon on the Mount, which gave him much stimulus, does not form the basis of his attitude, but only affirms something received long before.[37] For him the Indic doctrine of non-violence is plainly the one doctrine. Therefore he also believes it is present in all religions and binding for all men.

The most aggressive representative of Hinduism today is without question Radhakrishnan, who, armed with an astonishing amount of knowledge, tries to reconcile modern knowledge with Hinduism and to make it the coming world religion. He believes Hinduism gives the answer to all man's questions and therefore must be heard by all men. That would be so much the easier insofar as it is not exclusive and thus could unite all within itself. Radhakrishnan seeks to find in mysticism what is common to all religions. His importance for us, however, lies in the fact that he carries out the challenge to Christianity by summoning up a great knowledge of the history of dogma and attempts to demonstrate the derivation of Christianity from the Indic spiritual heritage. By reaching back to the Essenes and Enoch he believes he can prove that Jesus as the "Son of Man" adopted an Indic message."[38] In addition he interprets the passion of Jesus, his oneness with God, and the preaching of the kingdom of God as Indic. After he has drawn a comparision with Buddha, he summarizes: "Some of the noblest of the moral lessons usually supposed to be

---

[36] Wolff, *op. cit.*, p. 87.   [37] *Ibid.*, p. 69.
[38] S. Radhakrishnan, *Eastern Religions and Western Thought* (New York: Oxford University Press, 1959), pp. 157–187.

characteristic of Christianity are not characteristic of it alone. They are a necessary consequence of the spiritual life."[39] Naturally he lays the greatest emphasis upon the relation of Greek philosophy to Gnosticism on the one hand and the dependence of Christianity upon Gnosticism on the other hand.

> Christ answers to the Gnostic saviour god, the Logos and the Idea of the universe. . . . Jesus becomes the redeemed lord who is the source of salvation both in this world and in the world to come. The Messianic idea of the Jews gets mixed up with the Logos of the Greeks. . . . In St. Paul, Jesus becomes the centre of a cult where baptism and the commemoration of the Last Supper take the place of the sacraments of the mysteries.[40]

At every point Radhakrishnan seeks to prove that Christianity is nothing other than the result of Greek influences which have their origin in India. Proving this should serve to weaken the uniqueness of the Gospel and ascribe the originality, and thus the superiority, to Hinduism. Wolff thus sums up this criticism in his judgment: "No absolute uniqueness stands in the way of the desired total integration on the basis of Hinduism. Going beyond the sharpest critics of Christianity, Gandhi and Vivekananda, Radhakrishnan thrusts the challenging critique into the very center of the Christ picture. Ecce homo! What has become of this integrated Christ? Not only just one Avatar among many, but in no way a first-class Avatar."[41]

Islam

While Hinduism regards Christianity as a later variation of Hinduism, Islam declares it an earlier stage of Islam, a less valuable religion which has been surpassed by Islam as the perfected religion. The unique, comprehensive revelation is not the Holy Scripture, but the Koran, and in the last analysis the word of the Prophet. This belief is further outdone in the Ahmadiyya sect in that its founder Ahmad regarded himself as the universal savior, as the incarnation of Krishna, Buddha, Jesus,

---

[39] *Ibid.*, p. 175.   [40] *Ibid.*, pp. 233 ff.   [41] Wolff, "Wandlung . . . ," p. 104.

and Mohammed. Ahmad first gave real validity to the Koran.[42]
In contrast to the human form of the Bible, the Koran is the
unadulterated, pure, directly spoken word of God and therefore
perfect in everything. The Bible, on the other hand, has suffered
a loss of its authenticity through the many copies. While all
other religions have promised the coming word, the Koran contains the final word. The revelations of all peoples are brought
together in it. Therefore all religions must also be contained in
the Koran. Thus mankind receives a center from which it can
recognize God.[43] The New Testament must have been incorrect
to begin with, because Jesus spoke Hebrew but the congregations
repeated the word of Jesus from their memory in Greek. The
Koran on the other hand was sent directly from heaven and
this is unchanged. For these reasons Islam can never recognize
Christianity, but will always attempt to overcome the Christian
world. Islam proves the thesis that every post-Christian religion
must become an anti-Christian religion.

8. UNIVERSAL SIGNIFICANCE AND UNIVERSAL MISSION

The world religions today not only lay claim as national
religions upon the members of their own peoples, but they also
reach out for mankind and thus for Christians. They lay claim
to universal significance. Their claim is not just a reaction to
Christian missionary activity, but comes from the deep conviction that they have a better message than the Gospel. This sense
of superiority arose because of the lack of an example from
Western civilization and it will become the stronger the more the
moral collapse of the Western world, and thus of Christianity,
becomes apparent. Since the West has permitted materialism to
develop so shockingly that its one guiding principle seems to be
perfecting the standard of living, it can no longer offer men the
moral rallying point for which they yearn so intensely. Manikam
demonstrates how a cry for justice is going through mankind.

[42] Gottfried Simon, *Die Welt des Islam und ihre Berührungen mit der
Christenheit* (Gütersloh: Bertelsmann, 1948), p. 241.
[43] *Der Heilige Quran*, pp. 15 ff., 23 ff.

today.[44] Justice is no longer expected from the West. The Eastern religions, however, believe they can give mankind direction and strength here. They are convinced that they are superior as religions, and able to rescue mankind out of chaos. That is their driving power today. The motive is thus not salvation in the original sense, but help in the problems of life, which can lead to the self-salvation of mankind.

Hinduism

Vivekananda returned from Chicago with the conviction that only Indic mysticism could overcome Western materialism.[45] He founded the Ramakrishna Mission with the goal of making Hinduism a world religion, "a religion which could satisfy the highest religious aspirations and the most rigorous demands of mankind."[46] Vivekananda did not yet have in mind detaching persons from other religions, but was convinced that Hinduism was the crown of the religions, by which every other religion could be improved. "In this order one does not worry about the religious confession of the monk who joins. It is a matter of indifference whether he be a Christian, Hindu, or Buddhist."[47] It depends upon how one understands the deity. Vivekananda wanted to improve humanity by showing them a picture of man determined by the divine, an ideal Hinduism offered the power to realize. Through his mission the ideas of Hinduism seeped into the West.

Gandhi wanted to show modern man the way out of confusion. Hinduism was for him "a religion that could support and guide man in his efforts to solve the problems created by the modern situation."[48] But Gandhi went further than Vivekananda. Since he raised the doctrine of non-violence to the one valid principle,

[44] Ralph B. Manikam (ed.), *Christianity and the Asian Revolution* (Joint East Asia Secretariat of the International Missionary Council and the World Council of Churches, 1954), pp. 8–9.

[45] Wolff, *Indiens Beitrag . . .* , pp. 7 ff.

[46] Kulandran, *op. cit.*, p. 9.

[47] Jean Herbert, *Wege zum Hinduismus*, trans. Emma von Prelet (Zurich: Rascher, 1951), p. 117.

[48] Kulandran, *op. cit.*, p. 9.

he also made Hinduism the one valid and saving religion. Even he did not feel that all men should become Hindus, but he hoped that the other religions, especially Christianity, would allow themselves to be perfected by Hinduism. He wanted to ennoble the religions by means of Hinduism. Today it is primarily Swami Sivananda who understands himself to be the messiah and prophet of the new age, and believes he can rescue mankind through his "active mysticism."[49] Since Indian thinkers derive Christianity from India, Hinduism is held to be Christianity properly understood. Thus the infiltration of Christianity seems legitimate to the Indians. They believe that Hinduism alone can bring mankind peace in the international chaos. Even the Western followers of Hinduism have this goal in sight. Thus Brunton recommends that Yoga and meditation should be taught in the high schools.[50] The Hindus thus perceive a great political task for the religions. This will make their consciousness of mission even stronger.

Buddhism

A similar conviction prevails among Buddhists. They believe that the world in its present condition can only be helped by Buddha:

The alien nations that for long ruled over the Buddhist world have shrunk both morally and politically. The world is waiting for the message of the Buddha.[51]

Others believe that a new Buddha will come to bring peace and joy to the world . . . This and the growing fear of impending catastrophe in international affairs, coupled with the belief that Buddhism alone can save the world from doom [are the major foci of the discussion] . . . Many Buddhists feel that Christianity has failed to provide the potential for world peace.[52]

[49] Sri Swami Sivananda, *Dynamic Spiritual Awakening* (Calcutta), p. 37.
[50] Paul Brunton, *The Hidden Teaching Beyond Yoga* (New York: E. P. Dutton, 1941), p. 76.
[51] Kulandran, *op. cit.*, p. 19.
[52] Eastman, *op. cit.*, pp. 282–284.

It is said the Buddhist peoples never have reached for the sword; thus Buddhism can also bring peace to the world.

In the face of the moral collapse of the Christian nations of the West, Buddhism is claimed to provide the one way to lasting relationships of peace in the world.[53]

The Buddhist World Council was held in order to be able to fulfill this task. It gave to the total Buddhist world new motivation, the feeling of unity and of the importance of the missionary mandate:

A council is an occasion when the Buddhist world girds up its loins for the fight and lives on the stimulation for a long time after.[54]

Islam

Islam has always claimed universal significance and universal mission. It has always conceived itself to be the religion which has the mandate to bring mankind under the rule of Allah. The holy wars and the spontaneous spread of Islam are a proof of this. It cannot, to be sure, claim that it brings peace to the world, even though the peaceful uniting of mankind in Darul-Islam (the House of Islam) is its ultimate goal. In Islam, politics is the means toward reaching the goal of peace. "Islam is not only its [the Islamic world's] religion, but it is there that Islam has developed into the vast theological, socio-religious and cultural system which has enabled it to play so great a role in human history since the early Middle Ages."[55] Since religion and politics have the same goal, politics has always been regarded as the servant of religion. Thus even when Islam moves toward war, it claims as its ultimate goal the peace of mankind. Since on the basis of this position it would not greatly attract humanity today, the Ahmadiyya wants to spread Islam solely by peaceful means. Its awareness of mission, its need of world significance, and also its arrogance cannot be surpassed. It is proved from the Koran that Islam is the religion through which all mankind will be perfected.

[53] Kulandran, op. cit., p. 24.   [54] Ibid., pp. 19–20.
[55] Hendrik Kraemer, "The Christian Church in Non-Communist Muslim Asia," IRM, XLII (1953), 144.

It will establish an empire that will last eternally, uniting all peoples within itself. The history of Islam proves this.[56] It is a history of triumph over Christians to be completed by Ahmad and his followers. If the other religions proceed on the basis of mankind's longing for peace, Islam seeks to answer the cry for social justice. Through the eternal principles of Islam, a new society could be erected. Islam also seeks a common internal alignment and a common external effect. From year to year, conferences are held in Karachi in which representatives participate from all countries where Islam has taken root.

The world religions present their claim to universal significance, not on the basis of the question of salvation, but rather proceeding from the need of mankind. They promise to be able to help all. Thus the religions represent peoples who themselves are among those in need of help. Nevertheless this claim cannot be rejected as "presumption," for in it is a deep awareness of the fact that the world can only be helped if man is changed. These religions want to change man's attitude because then the external problems will also be eliminated.

[56] *Der Heilige Quran*, pp. 73–94.

3

The Missionary Object

1. THE RELIGIOUS CONTRAST

If we attempt to represent the Christian world as the missionary object of the world religions from the point of view of the religions, we must immediately point out several distinctions which are important to the understanding of this point of view.

We have classified the religions in a great variety of ways. If we wish to undertake a valid differentiation, we must begin with the God-relation, which always includes the understanding of man. Regarded from this point of view, Christianity and its great epigone, Islam, stand on one side. Both have in common the fact that they teach a personal God who is given to them through revelation. This God is Creator and Lord; man, however, is his opposite. Here there is no unity of God and man. God remains God and man remains man. The union occurs because man is God's creation and is under the authority of his creator. If he transgresses against God's will, he sins against God. Because God is the Lord, only God can save. According to Christian revelation man can be brought again into the right relation to God only through the redemptive death of Christ. Salvation is thus based upon forgiveness of sin and brought about by God alone. For Islam, however, salvation and forgiveness is already a humanization of God. Man can regret his sins, make atonement, and for the rest he remains totally cast upon the mercy of Allah. With respect to the world in both religions, man can only act to do the will of God and in so doing influence the world around him. Thus man remains the opposite of God, but he is always placed in a position of decision making and can therefore turn against Him. In this God-relation there is always the danger that man may become self-sufficient and, as a rebel against God, make himself his own master. Unfortunately that happened to a frightening degree in the older Christian world.

Hinduism and Buddhism know of no such personal God. In Buddhism theoretically there is no deity at all, but only an indefinable absolute power, from whose activity indeed the whole world proceeds in its various cycles, including the Buddha who belongs to every aeon. There is no actual being, otherwise world and man would also have to be realities. Man, however, is only the result of conditions of consciousness, which through his desires become united in self-consciousness. Therefore it is his task to dissolve himself again in his salvation. Here man must rely entirely upon himself. He knows no revelation. Buddha wanted only to show him one way to salvation, which, to be sure, is designated by the Buddhists as the only possible way to salvation. Man is here raised to master over himself, but on the other hand is held so strongly within his bounds that he always manifests himself in appearance as the one who denies his own existence. Through the way of Buddha he can throw off his illusory existence. The highest moral demands are made upon man in order to lead him back to non-existence. Duty in the world is negatively determined. It is given form more by what man does not do than by the good which is supposed to help him to salvation of self. Without question a damming up of evil takes place, which could also be present in Christianity if man would willingly subordinate himself to the commands of God. Thus, from its essential nature, Buddhism must become the greatest foe of Christianity.

Hinduism takes a middle position between Christianity and

Buddhism. It teaches faith in a divine power in the universe, but not in a personal God and Creator. There is no creation, but only a birth of the world. This is an emanation of the divine. Thus man also is understood as a part of the divine and as a result he must try to achieve an ever greater participation in the divine. Salvation always consists in being permeated by the divine and losing oneself in it. In seeking salvation, the individual may follow several paths. Either he becomes complete master, who of himself seeks the way to the divine, or he becomes a "fool of God" who is possessed by the divine and as a result no longer has any freedom of decision. In either case it is assumed that he can do good. At this point Christianity experiences the strongest injustice on the part of Hinduism. Since in Christianity man is the opposite of God, what man does cannot be laid as a burden upon God. That can be done, however, if God and man are regarded as one. In Hinduism and Buddhism men cannot sin against God, for they cannot transgress against a power which in the last analysis is the source of all activity. At most, one may sin against himself, but then this power is also responsible. Salvation can therefore not be reconciliation with God, but only redemption from the fateful union with evil. As the individual more and more discerns his own being, he will discover the divine in himself. Thus it is all up to the individual. From this point of view, the Christian faith is declared worthless, because through the Christian doctrine of redemption the action of man is excluded and no moral incentive exists. In addition the evil of men lies as a burden upon God. In Hinduism, on the other hand, the individual is completely determined by the divine. The Indic people today do not yet ask themselves whether it will always remain thus. Should such an emancipation of man take place as has happened in Christianity, as egoistical a man could result as has developed in the Christian countries.

From this basic attitude there comes a further difference. We are always reminded that the other religions have no organizational structure; Christianity on the other hand is organized in every detail. Even that is related to the intrinsic difference. The individual must be converted to the Christian God. Through baptism he becomes a member of the congregation. Christians are persons who have been called from the world and brought to God. They live in the world as members of the church of God. The other religions know no separate congregations of their own. What is present as a type of congregation in Buddhism is a union of the privileged few. In the non-Christian religions, community of religion and community of birth coincide. In them no question of faith is asked, no decision is demanded. One comes into the religion by birth, and not by conversion. Each member of the folk-group is carried by the tradition of the religion. At this point also, due to lack of understanding, criticism is leveled against Christianity. It is not understood that the congregation of God is something independent. Hence all crimes which its people commit are held against it and thus against Christianity. This criticism should warn against isolating the life of the church and stressing its organizations. In the other religions, each in his own position is responsible for what his religion demands of him. In Christianity, the individuals in the congregation no longer have an effect upon the world. For the most part they leave the responsibility to organizations which relieve the individual of his duty to witness. Hence the congregation cannot live out the Gospel. To be sure, Christianity needs its own forms of existence. If, however, through them the possibility of obedience is taken from the congregation, they harm the church.

In any case, if we listen to the reproaches in the following, it must be seen that something different is understood by "faith" in Christianity than in the other religions. Thus something different is understood by "apostasy." Particularly in Christianity, its consequences must be something bad. One should in no case count the apostates as members of the church. Brunton defined religion as the attempt of man to understand his life.[1] If that is all religion is, one cannot reproach it if it fails. It is then dependent on man. The Christian faith, on the contrary, is a relationship of trust in

[1] Paul Brunton, *The Hidden Teaching Beyond Yoga* (New York: E. P. Dutton, 1941), pp. 64-70.

God, and therefore Christianity must be blamed when man acts
against the will of God. Therefore we should learn to realize that
there is no faith without obedience. Christianity is judged today
according to the degree to which its members do the will of God.

2. THE DISILLUSIONING MODEL

The greatest disappointment for the peoples of Asia and Africa
was that the Gospel was so ineffective in the lives of its followers.
The non-Christian peoples are accustomed to seeing religion and
life as a unity and to judging religion by the lives of its followers.
A separation of religion from life, a limitation to the sphere of the
edifying, does not exist for them. Even the Lord Jesus said, "By
their fruits ye shall know them." On the basis of the way of
life of the white race, the judgment of the non-Christian
religions is unanimous: Christianity has failed! That is, to be
sure, a superficial, general judgment, but we should take it
seriously for the reason that it was through the failure of
Christianity that the religions found themselves and became
aware of their mandate to carry out missionary work among the
Christian peoples.

We shall first follow Thomas Ohm in discussing the criticism
of the West.[2] We must add, however, that in the meantime the
reproaches have increased significantly. His account says: The
Christians bring and sow division. They do not insure brotherhood. They always deal with others from above, and through
their arrogance have brought the race question into the world.
They love money. The whole colonization process rested on the
profit motive. Where the colonial powers put money into the
colonies, they did so only in order to take out more. Western
civilization is brutal. It aims always at the material progress of
the individual, who then oppresses others. Christians have an
exaggerated culture of the body. They have an immoderate sex
life. They are always interested in the material.

Brunton agrees with these utterances: Christians know only

[2] Thomas Ohm, *Asia Looks at Western Christianity*, trans. Irene Marinoff
(Edinburgh and London: Nelson, 1959).

technological, but not moral, progress. They are always concerned with technological perfection, but not with education and the growth of man in self-control.[3]

In this matter even the Ahmadiyya sets up a comprehensive comparison: Christianity of the first century did nothing for civilization. It did, however, bring a high culture. Today it brings civilization but little culture.[4]

Not even mentioned thus far are the two world wars, in the course of which the Christians showed themselves to be most brutal and ruthless men. In these wars the moral principles of Christianity were shown to be worthless. Thus the peoples lost any confidence they had in the white race. "The West set itself to explore the visible things of the world of the senses because the way to overcoming the world was hidden. Europe took no notice of spiritual India and satisfied itself with tangible conquests."[5]

Christianity, it is said, exhibits itself as the religion of force. Since the people of Asia reject coercion, they wish to have nothing further to do with the Gospel. "Whoever misuses his power to oppress others forgets that he is a slave to his lust for power. . . . In any case, man seeks endless fulfillment of his passions with pretty words."[6]

Another Japanese asked: "What is the meaning of the peculiar combinations which Europe brings about: hospital and torpedo, Christian mission and imperialism, the maintenance of enormous armaments as a guarantee of peace?"[7]

Worst, the Christian man even wants to embellish his actions morally and does not hesitate to give religious reasons for them. Behind everything he does, however, is not a religious spirit but

[3] Brunton, op. cit., p. 180.
[4] Der Heilige Quran: Arabisch-Deutsch, translated and with an extensive introduction by Hazrat Mirza Bashiruddin Mahmud Ahmad, et al. (Zurich and Hamburg: Ahmadiyya-Mission des Islams, 1954), p. 27.
[5] Hellmuth Hecker, "Der Buddhismus und das Abendland," Einsicht, 1957, p. 69.
[6] Masao Fukushima, Die Freiheit und der Glaube, trans. Osamu Yamada (Freiburg: K. Alber, 1956), p. 16.
[7] Jean Herbert, Wege zum Hinduismus, trans. Emma von Prelet (Zurich: Rascher, 1951), p. 19.

the spirit and tradition of man. On the basis of his experiences, Radhakrishnan writes: "The victory of Christianity over the life of the West has always been a remote vision, and the history of the Christian Church is the record of the gradual adaptation of an Eastern religion to the Western spirit. It is not the pale Galilean that has conquered, but the spirit of the West."[8]

Later we shall reconsider these criticisms, and we ought not just yet block the way to a thorough examination by indicating that much injustice and violence has also occurred among the non-Christian peoples. We should rather see that the people of the West have betrayed the mandate which they had from God. Was the colonial policy not ethically justified by the fact that the culturally superior people have a mandate from God to help those who are inferior? Thus Christianity has missed a one-time opportunity. Because of the disillusioning example of the Christians, the non-Christians' initial attraction to the Christian ideal has turned to vehement rejection. Today the non-Christian religions believe they must rescue mankind from Christianity.

3. NATIVE CULTURE CALLED IN QUESTION

At the World Missionary Conference in Ghana in 1957 and 1958, it was pointed out that the Eastern cultures are thoroughly marked by religion. The life of the mind which has filtered down into literature is religious through and through. Originally, religion determined to which social stratum a man belonged. Although based on the salvation of the individual, Hinduism and Buddhism strongly supported men's relationship to the kin group. In the community of fellow men lay social security. Religion shaped architecture, art, and music. Religion was the soul of culture.

The civilization brought by Western colonial government placed all that in question. The Western system of law necessarily conflicted with the conception of law of Eastern men, which was permeated by religion. European subjectivism recog-

---

[8] S. Radhakrishnan, *Eastern Religions and Western Thought* (New York: Oxford University Press, 1959), p. 271.

nizes only the individual personality. The European despised
the native culture and remained a stranger. He spread his civilization without taking religion into consideration. Western superiority in technology and industry necessarily loosed a feeling
of inferiority among the peoples. Feeling inferior always includes,
however, a longing for something higher in meaning, and therefore is the source of reaction. Since the way of life in Asia is
determined by religion, placing the culture in question necessarily
was construed as an attack upon religion. Raising Eastern man
to a higher standard of living was not possible without conflict
with the native culture, which should be conquered or surpassed.
Western science brought a secular conception of life.

The development also had its good side. It prepared many
men for their present tasks. The younger nations could neither
have won their freedom, nor could they have asserted it, had
this development not taken place. The Eastern peoples recognize
today, however, that under Western influence they are losing
the meaning of their life and that together with their culture
their humanity is being placed in question. Awakened by nationalism, they stand up for the preservation of their cultural
life. They live in an in-between state. On the one hand they
wish to be members of the great family of mankind, but on the
other hand they want to remain precisely what they have always
been. Since they have always known only a life determined by
religion, they seek even now to find through religion a synthesis
between civilization and their own culture. In religion they seek
the foothold which will enable them to stand up under the threat
of civilization. Since nothing is sacred to the white man, they
must protect themselves from him through their religion.

4. RELIGION PLACED IN QUESTION

Since the Western influences continually threatened the native
traditions, they necessarily appeared to be an attack upon religion. They were determined by a materialistic view of the
world. "Philosophical thought has developed in India in the
course of millennia, but it kept the even tenor of its way until

the British rule brought in its wake new forces of science and technology, democracy and nationalism, and the new philosophies—some of them idealistic, some of them realistic and pragmatic, some even sceptical, agnostic, atheistic and materialistic."[9] "Now it is experimentally based empiricism, criticism and ethic based on Kant, now it is technology, which presents the possibility of ways of life not heretofore extant, which controls the new educational establishments. 'The old teaching of the spirit has been lying more than a hundred years in the death struggle, and now it is dying,' thus Rabindranath Tagore looks back upon the positively radical disruptive influence which the entrance of the West brought with it."[10] "The modern world of the West seems to brush away four thousand years of spiritual tradition as if it were a mummified museum piece."[11] Islam likewise complains that the disintegration of Moslem tradition goes back to the influences of the West. The West did not do all this in order to overcome the religions, *but because it no longer had any religious bond itself.* Therefore it did not understand what religion meant for Asiatic men. The Ahmadiyya declares: Western teaching no longer bound men to God, hence arose the autonomous man.[12] The Bahai sect writes that had the Christians taken the teaching of Christ in earnest, there would be no need of religious renewal. Radhakrishnan sums everything up: "The prominence given to conation in psychology, pragmatism in philosophy, and social gospels in religion is leading us away from the inner life of the soul, the need for self-possession. It is an age in which power and speed are held to be more important than comprehension and love, an age of the tyranny and the futility of success. We are preoccupied with gospels of world affirmation, to the exclusion of world negation."[13]

The strongest attack on native religion was, without doubt, the Christian mission. It distinguished itself, however, from the other

[9] Dewan Bahadur K. S. Ramaswami Sastri, *Sivananda: The Modern World-Prophet* (Rishikesh: Yoga-Vedanta Forest University, 1953), p. 146.
[10] Wolff, *Indiens Beitrag zum neuen Menschenbild: Ramakrishna, Gandhi, Sri Aurobindo* (Hamburg: Rowohlt, 1957), p. 28. [11] *Ibid.*
[12] *Der Heilige Quran,* p. 29. [13] Radhakrishnan, *op. cit.,* p. 112.

Western influences insofar as it wanted to give men the right
relation to God. Today the Asiatics scarcely make a distinction
between Western unbelief and Christian mission. Both attack
their religion, therefore both are harmful. Even unbelief is laid
at the door of the mission. So much harmful influence derives
from Christianity that it has no right to carry on missionary
activity.[14] The mission is the rejection and violation of the other
religions. Every mission is in danger of religious imperialism. Since
the mission has often depended upon world events, it is accused
of being an instrument of the Western drive for expansion. At
the same time, the effort is made to base all this upon the content
of the Christian faith. The claim that Jesus alone is the Savior
of mankind is an enormity and is not in accordance with the
Gospel. "Unfortunately Christian religion inherited the Semitic
creed of the 'jealous God' in the view of Christ as 'the only be-
gotten son of God'. . . . When Europe accepted the Christian
religion, in spite of its own broad humanism, it accepted the fierce
intolerance which is the natural result of belief in 'the truth
once for all delivered to the saints.' Finality of conviction easily
degenerates into the spirit of fanaticism, autocratic, over-positive,
and blood thirsty."[15] Thus the missionary activity of the Christian
church and the claim to lordship of Jesus Christ was marked as
a great presumption.[16] As we see, even here the question of the
truth does not stand behind these reproaches, but only Asiatics'
desire to rescue their own religions. Since today the world religions have gone over to missionary activity, it is to be hoped
that their peoples will find a more just judgment of Christian
missionary work.

5. UNBELIEF

The Asiatic today is concerned to understand how the situation can have gone so far in Christianity that its people no longer
work constructively within society, but destructively. Christianity is reproached that she has become the mother of unbelief,

[14] Ohm, *op. cit.*, pp. 201 ff.   [15] Radhakrishnan, *op. cit.*, p. 324.
[16] Ohm, *op. cit.*, pp. 35 ff.

which cannot be said of any other religion. From the Christian countries have come forth the irreligious movements of secularism, materialism, and communism. These people would naturally not recognize that it cannot be otherwise in Christianity.· Jesus Christ is indeed not only the critic, but at the same time the end of the religions. There is no way beyond him. One can only fall away from Jesus Christ and change oneself into the opposite of *homo religiosus*. The non-Christian, if he is dissatisfied with his religion, seeks for something better and thus becomes more pious. The apostate Christian, on the other hand, can only leave religion behind. Thus in the last analysis the ideological movements must be the proof that Jesus is the unique one upon whom no one can improve. Therefore, when men turn from Jesus Christ, they can only turn against Him. This is already becoming clear in the non-Christian religions as well.·

Naturally one could say that the reproach that Christianity is to blame for the development of the world today does not strike home because it is those who have fallen away from Christianity, or who are indifferent to it, who have brought about the state of affairs in the world. This excuse is too cheap, however. We must ask ourselves here how it happens that such movements develop out of Christianity. The answer of the Asiatic peoples touches a sore spot of our church life. Christianity has not understood how to unite and to shape its people. It is a religion of the individual, which knows no responsibility for fellow men. Thus Christians are not supported by the community of Christians. They do not subject themselves to any tradition which gives them stability.

From these observations the Asiatic peoples derive the powerlessness of Christianity. They examine the objective facts to see what religion means for Western men. One does not see Westerners pray, hence their religion has no place in life.[17] Asiatics pray a great deal, and are therefore better men. When Europeans pray they bring forth a mass of petitions, while the Asiatics turn

[17] *Ibid.*, p. 116.

within and collect themselves in prayer. Since one sees so little
of religion in the lives of the white race, God is for them only
a transcendent being without influence upon daily life. The white
race has, indeed, not yet grasped the heart of religion. Radhakrishnan presents the harshest indictment of Christianity: "We
are familiar with the story of the clergyman who asked the captain of the ship, when a storm broke out, what he was doing.
The captain said: 'We have done all we could and now we can
only trust in God.' The clergyman replied: 'Is it as bad as all
that?' "[18] Thus the Western man calls it bad when God, who
alone can help, must help. God stands on the edge of activity and
not at the origin. Therefore he cannot determine the life of
men. One needs God only when nothing else is possible. This is
in complete opposition to the spirit of the Asiatic man. For him
the divine is the formative factor. Thus Gandhi could once say of
the Soviets, "They have deposed God, then no form of socialism
can help."[19]

The worst criticism is that Christianity scarcely recognizes its
spiritual degeneracy and for this reason more and more falls prey
to it. "In Christianity not only have the capabilities disappeared,
which Christ and his disciples and highly inspired men had . . .
but it has become blind as Hodur (the blind Hodur killed and
misled his half brother unintentionally.) Buddhism still knows
a way to awaken people to God. Christianity no longer strives
for this awakening."[20] According to Erich Schmidt, Christianity
has suffered the fate of all organized religions. They want to
prescribe what religion is, but then it no longer has any place
in life. "The more fixed a religion becomes, the further it stands
from the original spirit out of which it was born. Commentaries
are the end of a religion."[21]

It is significant that many see the basis for the immobility of
Christianity in Christian anthropology, at a point therefore where
the Christian conception differs most strongly from that of the

---

[18] Radhakrishnan, *op. cit.*, p. 60.   [19] Wolff, *op. cit.*, p. 66.
[20] Hellmut von Schweinitz, *Buddhismus und Christentum* ("*Glauben und
Wissen*," *Nr.* 14 [Munich: Ernst Reinhardt, 1955]), p. 33.
[21] Erich Schmidt, "Die Welt ohne Vorstellung," *Einsicht,* 1957, p. 8.

heathen religions. Because man is understood as a sinner by
nature, he is held incapable of anything good and any striving
toward noble ends on his own. Therefore he trusts in "cheap
grace." "As a consequence of Adam's disobedience, it is impossible for sinful man to fulfill the moral law by his own effort
and attain salvation. For St. Paul 'flesh and blood cannot inherit
the kingdom of God'... The complete depravity of man gives
the opportunity for the divine plan of salvation through Christ.
... For the orthodox Christian, the coming of the Kingdom of
God is catastrophic and not the peaceful outcome of an ever-
widening process of evolution; that is, an intervention of God
right *into* history and not springing *from* it."[22] Here then the
action of Christians and their unbelief are in the last analysis
traced back to God and laid at the door of the Christian doctrine
of salvation. Because this essential core is false, Christianity
cannot contribute to improving the world. The right spirit is not
present, which would lead men to an inner stability.

Just as the acts of the white race are ascribed to God, they are
also ascribed to his revelation, the Gospel, and to its carrier, the
church. The church hides the Gospel; therefore it can exert no
further influence. Christianity exhausts itself today in churchi-
anity.[23] The many church rules, church customs, and secondary
concerns do not allow the Word of God to be effective. The
Christian today is satisfied with results, but no longer lives by the
word of God. Mankind can no longer see Christ because He is
hidden by the church. In addition, the church concerns itself far
too little with the real person. Through its compassion for the ill,
the weak, the deprived, and the damned, Christianity has become
a religion for those who somehow are thrust outside of society. The
normal person, however, would receive no guidance and stimulation from it. From these facts comes the dead-end future of the
white race. The other religions, on the other hand, leave their
stamp upon man.

"What thus distinguishes the main religions are not so much
their moral laws and ethical rules of conduct but rather the goal

---

[22] Radhakrishnan, *op. cit.,* pp. 73–74.   [23] Ohm, *op. cit.,* pp. 46–47.

that they set up for mankind and the methods they prescribe for reaching this goal ... In all countries there rules a desperate yearning for peace. But peace as well as war arise in the spirit of man. Many men the world over are beginning to realize that this problem of attaining peace is the decisive one even for the individual."[24] For example, love of one's neighbor in Christianity is "a command of God and the whole Christian ethic is rooted in this command, which man can keep, but also cannot keep. In the command as such there lies the danger that it is kept only to please God ... The morality of love however becomes totally undermined whenever it binds itself to the idea of a reward in heaven or in a later life, reward in the sense of happiness. That is transcendent eudaemonism of the hereafter over which happiness hovers as the motive and goal of all endeavor."[25]

Even more radical in its criticism is Islam. The Quran tries to prove that mankind cannot observe God's law because Jesus designated the law as a curse.[26] Thus Christianity leads men away from God. Islam, however, leads to God. "Christian teaching frees mankind from all restrictions and espouses the position that God's law cannot lead mankind to moral behavior. Man took from God, so to speak, the duty to devise his own plans for his salvation. The result was that the same religion according to which the sacrifice of God was necessary to the salvation of man, now began to spread the teaching that guidance from God was not necessary for the further moral development of man."[27] "It is astonishing that Christians believe that the sinful heart is cleansed by the belief in the crucifixion of Jesus, but deny the truth that a repentant sinner will achieve the forgiveness of his Lord. And still we see that in everyday life the Christians do not seem to know the dogma of the atonement ... It could now be asserted that the belief in the crucifixion is equivalent to the purification of the heart. Meanwhile the behavior of Christians

---

[24] "Ein Staatsmann erklärt den Buddhismus," *Einsicht*, 1956, p. 17.
[25] Max Ladner, "Über die Nächstenliebe," *Einsicht*, 1956, p. 169.
[26] *Der Heilige Quran*, pp. 30 ff.   [27] *Ibid.*, p. 29.

the world over contradicts it. The evil and vice which infect the Christian countries are difficult to find in other parts of the world."[28]

The causes for the ineffectiveness of the Gospel are sought repeatedly in anthropology and in the doctrine of grace. In the latter, the non-Christian man sees questioned his moral striving to save himself. He cannot understand that his status as a human being does not count, and as a result he misunderstands the Gospel to read as if grace had made the law invalid, while it is precisely grace which is the guarantee that God's law remains in force. Otherwise the exercise of grace would not be necessary. The non-Christian man also does not understand that grace places man at the point of decision.

In interpreting the doctrine of grace, do the other religions not make the same mistake of which they accuse Christianity? They judge everything by reason and do not recognize that faith, love, and hope constitute completely different values, which reason cannot grasp. The deepest criticisms against the Gospel come from the fact that reason is not recognized in it, whereas reason finds a place in the other religions.

Naturally the ideological movements as they come from the West are felt as a great threat by the religions. Already through the spirit of materialism, money has become a god for many people today even in Asia and Africa. Secularism is not spread only by the West, but also by the educated of their own peoples. Communism is taken up by the impoverished as a messianic message. The peoples feel they are delivered up to these currents, hence the battle against Western unbelief.

"Modern civilization with its scientific temper, humanistic spirit, and secular view of life is uprooting the world over the customs of long centuries and creating a ferment of restlessness."[29] This means that modern unbelief stems, not from the people, but from the educated, who have never found the synthesis between faith and knowledge. Man does not consist only of intellect, however, nor the world only of mathematically expressible laws. As in

[28] *Ibid.*, p. 143.   [29] Radhakrishnan, *op. cit.*, p. vii.

man there are still other characteristics, so also in the world of
research there are still powers which we can only intuit, but
which represent the harmony of the world. Since they cannot be
grasped by the senses, however, the tangible world is set up as
absolute. Even the Asiatic thinkers see this. "The present crisis in
human affairs is due to a deep crisis in human consciousness, a
lapse from the organic wholeness of life. There is a tendency to
overlook the spiritual and to exalt the intellectual."[30] Ramakrishna
has said this in the sharpest possible words. "Religion is experience, lives on experience, without experience is noise and smoke,
intellectual monomania. The root of argumentative religious
intellectualism, which only turns knowledge here and there with
mere words, is egotism, which wants to assert itself in the uncom-
mittedness of mere talk... The merely learned are vultures. They
are carrion vultures which hover far above, but their eyes are
fastened upon the carrion in the garbage pit, upon advantage,
value, pride and worse."[31] Since Western men take the results
of science for themselves without at the same time entering into
a religious bond and without completing science with religious
experience, they fall prey to the objective subjectivism which
excludes God from their activity. They simply have not understood that no science can furnish an ethical norm. Our development is a proof for the fact that it is not enough when man sets
himself as the norm. He never does this as a species, but always
as an individual; he then becomes a danger to others.

6. THE DESTRUCTIVE RELIGION

On the basis of the above, Christianity is then felt to be the
destructive religion against which mankind must be warned.
The Ahmadiyya even presents it as anti-Christian. "The contemporary church is the anti-Christ foretold 'by the prophets' which
claims to exist in the name of Jesus Christ, but in reality stands
in diametrical opposition to the teachings of Jesus."[32] The asser-

[30] *Ibid.*, p. 38.   [31] Wolff, *op. cit.*, p. 30.
[32] Gottfried Simon, *Die Welt des Islam und ihre Berührungen mit der
Christenheit* (Gütersloh: Bertelsmann, 1948), p. 246.

tion that Christianity can no longer fulfill its duties is based on
the fact that the Europeans themselves have rejected the
Gospel,[33] which leads one to ask how the actions of the Europeans
can be charged against Christianity. Church history is the history
of the betrayal of the teachings of Christ. Christianity has
nurtured the Western type of conqueror. The race laws are the
best proof that the Christians have not accepted the other
peoples into their community. They also do not care to maintain
peace. "Christianity was an ally of capitalism and imperialism
and is an instrument for oppressing weaker nations."[34] "The
western races were not prepared to abandon the world [in the
Biblical sense] or look upon its ends as impermanent. Their
energies were too great, the natural man in them unsubduable
... Religion is employed to sanctify human passions. The tragedy
of man is keenest when his love of power puts on the garb of
spiritual dignity. Of all fetters, worldliness assuming the garb of
religion is the most difficult to break."[35]

From this point of view the sharpest judgments are leveled
against the Christian mission. It is associated with the Western
urge toward expansion. "Their [the Western people's] desire for
world domination transformed the simple faith of Jesus into a
fiercely proselytizing creed."[36] Panikkar claims to present proof
that mission and politics go hand in hand. Either the mission
came as a result of colonial power, or the colonial power used the
presence of the mission in order to extend its domination.
Prudently Panikkar remains quiet about all examples where
colonial power hindered missionary activity. Also nothing is said
about the fact that the mission often carried on bitter battles
against the colonial power for the benefit of the natives. India
would well afford examples for this. Radhakrishnan recognizes
that missionary activity has benefited India. Nevertheless he
continues: "But is this efficiency the expression of religion? ...

[33] Ohm, *op. cit.*, p. 47.
[34] Kavalam Madhiva Panikkar, *Asia and Western Dominance: A Survey
of the Vasco da Gama Epoch of Asian History 1498–1945* (London: George
Allen & Unwin, 1953), p. 451.
[35] Radhakrishnan, *op. cit.*, pp. 271–272.   [36] *Ibid.*, p. 10.

The New Testament tells us that it is not possible to serve both God and Mammon, and yet we are told that material prosperity is the chief criterion of success and that material rewards mean moral virtue."[37] Worst are the reproaches in African books. Christianity has only added one more god to Africa's four hundred gods. In addition, Christianity appears in such disunion that a searching non-Christian does not know which church he should join.

On the other hand the non-Christian religions seek to improve Western man. They claim (with the exception of Islam) that they do not want to win the Christians for themselves, but they want to make better Christians. They sense that in this confused world situation no religion has *the* word. Therefore all religions must complete themselves. We know that even Toynbee espouses these ideas. Viewing our world which has been changed by science, Brunton proposes the same thing: "It [religion] should add new beliefs, or alter and adapt its system whenever needed. It must progress parallel with the intellect of man, be on the move with our moving age, and not remain an inflexibly obstinate creed."[38] However—would not the intractable spirit of man achieve supremacy right here, and subordinate religion to itself? Could the Gospel then still be God's message for men?

[37] *Ibid.*, p. 322.   [38] Brunton, *op. cit.*, p. 381.

4

The Message of the Religions

1. THE NEW UNDERSTANDING OF THE WORLD

What do the Eastern religions then actually offer
Western man? With what do they seek to answer his questions?
By what means do they appeal to so many Western men? These
questions can only be answered by implication, but in so doing
we reach a startling conclusion. The religions bring no relief for
external conditions of need upon which we in the West lay so
much stress. Their adherents know that behind every social
question stands a religious question. They go into these. They
also recognize that man, irrespective of whether he is an intellectual or a simple worker, lives under a mere mask of materialism; inwardly, he seeks for the basic principles of his life. They
know something more: The world cannot achieve peace unless
man is changed, his heart transformed and his thinking given a
new direction. They do not want to help the external distress, but
to eliminate the internal one; then the external disappears of
itself.

"Men confusedly yearn for an outlook, or put differently, for
'spiritual peace' or 'rest.' "[1] What U Nu says about all mankind is
without question valid for Western man, who suffers more than

[1] "Ein Staatsmann erklärt den Buddhismus," *Einsicht,* 1956, p. 18.

he inwardly admits to himself under spiritual fragmentation and homelessness, under the tension of fear and hope. Western man perceives exactly as does Eastern man that wealth and technology can give him no supporting answer, even though he strives for these things because he still does not know how he can become spiritually independent of them. "East and West have the same human nature, a common human destiny, the same striving toward a greater perfection, the same seeking for something that is higher than East and West, which we strive for not only inwardly, but also in external things."[2]

This insight is so difficult for us to grasp because we no longer ascribe any importance to spiritual things and obstruct the way to true man. Wolff analyzes this:

Contemporary Western man, secularized and made into a mass man, standardized and made a part of a technological system, without metaphysical basis and without a genuine love-relationship, depersonalized and robbed of personality, shares that condition of consciousness which is crusted over by rationalism even where he still is in the central Christian or inner church sphere.[3]

Western man fails to establish a relationship between what he believes and his everyday life. Hinduism appeals to him at this point of inadequacy. It gives man again the deep sense of unity with the world in which he must live. It explains the world as the place where the divine is at work and today points out to man a duty in the service of the divine. The Indian can no longer deal with the world as "Maya," i.e., the world of appearance. He has filled the concept with so much new meaning that the world becomes the historical sphere of duty for man. In it man can fulfill his duty as an instrument of the divine.

The phenomenal character of the empirical self and the world answering to it is noted by the word *maya*, which signifies the fragility of the universe. *Maya* does not mean that the empirical world with the selves in it is an illusion, for the whole effort of the cosmos is

[2] Otto Wolff, *Indiens Beitrag zum neuen Menschenbild: Ramakrishna, Gandhi, Sri Aurobindo* (Hamburg: Rowohlt, 1957), p. 11.   [3] *Ibid.*, p. 9.

directed to and sustained by the one supreme self, which though distinct from everything, is implicated in everything. The criticism that Hindu thought is pantheistic makes out that the supreme being, which is complete and impenetrable, is yet filled with things which live, breathe, and move each according to its nature. Nothing can be born, exist, or die in any degree, nothing can have time, place, form or meaning, except on this universal background.[4]

Maya is not an "illusion" wherein moral endeavour is laid in question. Space and time may not be ultimately real, but they represent a "phase" of Reality. *Maya* implies that this world of experience is a mixture of truth and illusion, a complex of the eternal and temporal, positing an element of indeterminism in the world process which demands choice in human conduct, thus making life in the here and now worth living.[5]

Here the world (and with it mankind) is not regarded as set free over against the divine to be an arena for man's selfish activity; on the contrary, the divine works in the world and makes men his instruments. Man does not stand between two fronts. He does not confront God with His unchanging will on the one side and the world with its harsh demands on the other side. Everything is seen as a great harmonious whole. The divine guarantees the meaning of events even though the world appears upset. The earlier monism of India is thus deepened. Man is not isolated, as though he had to stand outside the world in order to become one with the divine. Only the great cosmic process remains, which develops according to divine intentions; man is responsible for what happens only insofar as he can keep aloof from the divine. This new understanding of the world in Hinduism makes it possible for man both to influence the world and to live under the influence of a higher power.

The security of man here no longer lies in faith, i.e., in trust in an otherworldly power, but in a feeling of unity with everything that lives. In this both destiny and an outlook on life are

[4] S. Radhakrishnan, *Eastern Religions and Western Thought* (New York: Oxford University Press, 1959), p. 27.
[5] Ralph B. Manikam (ed.), *Christianity and the Asian Revolution* (Joint East Asia Secretariat of the International Missionary Council and the World Council of Churches, 1954), p. 132.

given. Thus a decision of faith in the strict sense is no longer necessary. That is very attractive to modern man. We shall deal with these ideas later.

It is significant that similar ideas have become prominent in Buddhism.

Faith has its root in our uncertainty and fear. Faith strengthens us in this transitory and sorrowful life. It gives us a hope for the future. We project this hope upon everything that we see and everything proves to us the correctness of our faith. We may be inclined to admit that the Christian faith in all forms is worthless, especially the belief in the life after death, in reward and punishment in heaven and hell. Thus it is, however, with everything of which we know nothing. Such faith does not work upon our lives in a transforming fashion . . . It is a way of flight into false reassurance, and herein lies its destructive quality.

Religion means the discovery of truth, of reality; religion is not faith in something somehow known or given; religion is not the search for truth.

Life consists of relationships; religion is life in relation to others . . . Whoever withdraws from this world today in order to find peace in a lonely place acts against active living. He will find no peace . . .[6]

To be sure, up until now there is no theistic principle in Buddhism, but the monistic principle is already present. This is man himself, who suffers with the world and is called to her help. Brunton believes he can offer a way out here. He establishes first of all the principle that India today demands its tribute from the rest of the world, in order to then develop a philosophy of perfect Yoga which is completely Indic and gives full value to monism. He says that everything which is outside the body is only perceived as reality because man through his organs of sense transmits it to his spirit which recognizes it as reality. Things would thus not be there, would have no existence, if the recognizing spirit did not exist. Perception and recognition are therefore conditions of our consciousness, in which, however, matter and spirit become one. Thus the material object is always given

[6] Erich Schmidt, "Die Welt ohne Vorstellung," *Einsicht*, 1956, pp. 4, 6–7.

form by our spirit. Nothing then remains, neither God nor world. Man is the ultimate unity, having a spirit which is a part of the world-spirit. He is the final instance for everything. Man is thereby rescued. He can no longer be called to account.[7]

2. THE NEW UNDERSTANDING OF MAN

With the new understanding of the world a new understanding of man is also given. Just as the world is filled with the divine, so also is man. Since man is a thinking and feeling creature, however, there arise here the great questions of human existence. The religions under discussion have a simple answer. They do not trouble themselves with the questions of theodicy or with the *deus absconditus*. For them the divine is basically good. They therefore avoid the real answer. Even when the divine continuously works in the world it apparently achieves only good. Whence comes evil, misfortune? The religions must not ask themselves these questions pointedly because they ascribe to evil no power over man. There is, to be sure, the devil, the tempter, but in the last analysis he cannot determine destiny.

In Hinduism the existence of man is always explained axiomatically by the postulates of the transmigration of the soul and of retribution, and thus the teaching about evil is brought into a unique relationship with human existence. On the basis of this teaching, man has no one-time existence; his present existence is a result of the previous existences. Through samsara he again comes into existence; through karma he comes into a specific form of existence. Life is a continual becoming and passing away. "As a result, for the Hindus the soul is the element of permanence, the absolute, which is subject to no change and is removed from the contingencies of time, of space and of causality."[8]

The soul is eternal, but man himself is transitory and he has to bear the consequences of his karma. The eternal law "Whatever a man sows, that he will also reap" rules the world in karma.

[7] Paul Brunton, *The Hidden Teaching Beyond Yoga* (New York: E. P. Dutton, 1941), pp. 206–207, 297, 299–300, 357–358.
[8] Jean Herbert, *Wege zum Hinduismus,* trans. Emma von Prelet (Zurich: Rascher, 1951), p. 101.

Karma is thus not a capricious fate, but eternal justice:

> Karma means the unique, eternal, primordial form, which represents
> itself in its own Self . . . Man grasps through spiritual contemplation
> of Karma the unending primordial Self.
> Karma is pre-existence or the consequence of previous acts. It is the
> result of life activities which have been stored up.
> Karma differs from fate. The latter means that external powers are
> at work. In Karma, however, the act of one's own power is central.[9]

> The so-called Fate is only our past Karma which we can effectively
> counteract through a new Karma blessed by God's grace. If blind
> destiny rules, then there is no significance in ethical commandments,
> which imply that we have a right of choice in our actions.[10]

Thus it is man who brings himself forward in his reincarnations,
but according to the law of cause and effect. The present life is
a result of his previous existence.

Hinduism and Buddhism agree in the belief in karma. No
variation affects the basic concept. This teaching is also present
in concealed form in Islam.[11] It is surprising, however, that the
teaching of reincarnation and recompense also makes a deep impression on Western man. It is for him an explanation of his life.[12]
Today this Indic philosophical heritage is promulgated more
strongly than ever in the West by the teaching of Yoga. Brunton
points out that the teaching of karma assures us of continuity of
history.[13] Man is the product of his past. That gives him an explanation of his existence and it is a moral impetus to provide
a better form for the next life. Actually man today yearns for

---

[9] Masao Fukushima, *Die Freiheit und der Glaube*, trans. Osamu Yamada
(Freiburg: K. Alber, 1956), pp. 30 and 36.
[10] Dewan Bahadur K. S. Ramaswami Sastri, *Sivananda: The Modern
World-Prophet* (Rishikesh: Yoga-Vedanta Forest University, 1953), p. 28.
[11] E. L. Dietrich, "Die Lehre von der Reinkarnation im Islam," *Zeitschrift für Religions—und Geistesgeschichte* (hereafter referred to as *ZRGG*),
1957, p. 129.
[12] Ernst Benz, "Die Reinkarnation in Dichtung und Philosophie der
deutschen Klassik und Romantik," *ZRGG*, 1957, p. 150. See also Christmas
Humphreys, *Buddhism* (Harmondsworth: Penguin Books, 1958), pp. 230–
231.
[13] Brunton, *op. cit.*, pp. 384 ff.

such an explanation. He wants to know why his present life must be lived in precisely this way. On the other hand, he scarcely concerns himself about the next reincarnation.

Most men do not make clear to themselves, however, that nothing is explained with karma. Aurobindo has done us the great service of proving this. According to Wolff, he says that with karma neither natural catastrophes nor historical occurrences can be explained, nor can innocent suffering. The law of karma is only a vulgarization of human methods. It always concerns itself only with the individual. Salvation is atomized. In addition, the teaching offers no comfort, for even if I rise higher in the next incarnation, I can never know it, because I know nothing of the preceding life. It is teleologically understood, but no one can say whether it really works thus. It is not clear to the common man that even according to Indian judgment, fate cannot be explained by the teaching of karma, neither personal fate, for no one knows his previous existences, nor common fate, for it has no room for peoples, history, humanity, community—in short, for collective guilt.[14]

The religions promise a way out of karma. This is so obvious to Western man that it already belongs to the common understanding. Man is basically good and has a free will. He can find his way out of karma through the good he increasingly does. The Ahmadiyya goes so far as to insist: If man cannot distinguish between good and evil, neither can God. Man is thus made equal to God.[15] It is similar in the other two religions. "Human nature is fundamentally good and the spread of enlightenment will abolish all wrong. Vice is only a miss, an error. We can learn to become good. Virtue is teachable."[16] One is here reminded of the words of Vivekananda: "You divinities on earth! Sinners? It is a sin to call a man this; it is a defamation of human nature . . . You

[14] Otto Wolff, "Das Problem der Wiedergeburt nach Sri Aurobindo," *ZRGG*, 1957, pp. 116 ff.
[15] *Der Heilige Quran: Arabisch-Deutsch*, translated and with an extensive introduction by Hazrat Mirza Bashiruddin Mahmud Ahmad, *et al.* (Zurich and Hamburg: Ahmadiyya Mission des Islams, 1954), p. 22.
[16] Radhakrishnan, *op. cit.*, p. 3. He is discussing the Greek position.

are not bodies, matter is your servant, you are not the servants of matter!"[17]

Buddhism does not say it in this fashion, but means the same.

Buddha teaches: Man belongs to himself! The self is master of the self! The creative power which bore him is his own activity. Buddha calls living beings "wombs of activity." Man's own activity sits in judgment over him and his existence depends on his activity.[18]

The central aspect of Buddhism is not a divine being, but man. He alone is master of his fate and for all his speaking, doing and thinking he alone is responsible.[19]

According to Brunton, man must ask himself not "Who am I?" but "What am I?" Then he will recognize his involvement with the world, and he will be prompted to find the way out of karma.[20] About the way itself, the religions teach differently. They are agreed, however, that man can find the way. He should not look to an external power, but to himself. The more he acquires basic recognition of himself through meditation, the more he will recognize that everything that has an origin also has an end.[21] Then he will succeed in coming out of his human existence. "Physical death is something unavoidable—a mechanical process. The death of the ego is our original spiritual deed—a creative process which leads out of the birth of the timeless moment into deathlessness."[22] It is otherwise in Hinduism, where there is no liberation without religion and thus no salvation apart from the divinity. While in Buddhism salvation explicitly concerns itself with eliminating ignorance concerning the real being of man, Ramakrishna emphasizes recognizing the second ego, i.e., the divine in man, and allowing it to act. He can say: "To be is higher than to know." According to him the man who loves God is the man freed from himself. If all derives from the second ego,

[17] S. R. Yesudian, *Yoga* (Zurich, 1955), p. 16. Cf. Everett L. Cattell, "The Christian Impact on India," *IRM*, LI, 157.
[18] Soma Thera, "Eine Weltanschauung für unsere Zeit," *Einsicht*, 1956, p. 75.   [19] Max Ladner, "Buddhismus," *Einsicht*, 1956, p. 86.
[20] Brunton, *op. cit.*, p. 22.   [21] Ladner, *op. cit.*, p. 84.
[22] Schmidt, *op. cit.*, p. 4.

everything, including the individual's act, is referred back to the divine, and thus all doubt is removed. For Aurobindo, man and the divine stand beside one another. In contemplation of the divine, in listening to the divine, in his own stepping aside, man becomes free because the divine is brought into the center. Thereby man becomes whole man; indeed, there arises the superman who has become the vessel of the divine.

When we look over these statements it occurs to us that it is never a matter of the divine itself in this, but always a matter of man. The determining factor is primarily not what God wishes, but what man must do in order to fulfill himself. Man is always to be saved. He shall become master over himself, then he can unveil the puzzle of the world. Behind this effort of man stands a great earnestness with a high goal. Even here the differences between the divine and the human are erased.

> Those who realize that every soul belongs to God cannot help working for the divinization of the world. The great march of humanity towards the far-off divine ideal is directed and held together in the central lines by the effort and example of the saints, who are the natural leaders of mankind.[23]

Islam does not teach unity with God, but the difference between God and man. No man can have God at his disposal, as is the case in the Indic religions. In relation to God, man can only be a slave. Man must maintain the law of Allah completely. It is not doubted at all that man can do this. If he fails to do it, he can repent. Through virtue and good works he can make up for errors. For Islam, therefore, salvation through Jesus Christ is unacceptable. The law is decisive. Through it mankind receives a focal point: God! The better men keep the law, the closer they come to this focal point. Although Islam binds its people to Allah through the law, nevertheless the claim of man is here maintained. He need not allow himself to be saved. He works out his own salvation through obedience and good works. He remains master!

[23] Radhakrishnan, *op. cit.*, p. 54.

As a free man the Asiatic is directed to his fellow human beings, i.e., to such as likewise have a share in the divine. Here man is not regarded so much as a member of a sociological group, but rather in his participation in God. From this point of view it follows that consideration must be given to fellow men. Even in Buddhism where compassion for all forms of life is preached, these ideas ultimately stand in the foreground. Here social activity is based in the religions. It is an emanation of the divine which works in the individual man. Man thus finds his consummation in the divine.

3. THE NEW CONCEPT OF GOD

From all of this it follows that the concept of God in these religions must always proceed from the concept of man. Since Hinduism and Buddhism acknowledge no transcendent God, they cannot in the final analysis speak of revelation. In their view, knowledge about God must always be determined by the connection between cause and effect. Therefore it is always immanent knowledge. Man does not allow himself to be told through revelation who God is and what he himself is: rather, he gains his understanding of himself, from which also comes his understanding of God, through clarification of the question of existence. Since Eastern man is bound by the teaching of reincarnation and retribution, he carries his yearning for the eternal into his understanding of himself. He seeks the absolute, an existence not subject to these laws. He believes if he comes into contact with the eternal he, too, will be freed from temporality. The concept of God must therefore be determined completely by human experience.

This man can conceive of no other God but such as can be understood by reason. Therefore God does not stand outside human consciousness, but remains contained therein. Although all the religions under discussion proceed from postulates, there is in them no belief in a pre-existing God. They insist they have no teachings about God, but that everyone has the right and the duty to "identify" God anew. Therefore Hinduism and Buddhism claim only to be ways to God. In both of them human ability to comprehend is the ultimate measure for that which they call "the absolute." That suits the natural man. Here he need make no decision. Nothing is prescribed for him. His relation to God corresponds to his own understanding.

Buddhism proceeds most radically here in that, postulating that there can be no empiric being, it also denies the existence of a higher power. It allows the divinities to remain, but to the Buddhist they are only higher forms of rebirth. Most recently, however, Buddhists have turned more toward the idea of an absolute. "God is only a name which those gave and give to their ignorance who resign upon the way to the truth or who declare the search for truth to be presumptuous and arrogant and who declare this to be 'reverence before the inscrutable.' "[24]

On the other hand, among the Buddhists much emphasis is placed upon the fact that Buddha's knowledge corresponds to science and as a result needs no further justification.[25]

Some Buddhists advocate Buddhism as the only scientific religion. According to them Buddhism rejects all superstition, and the belief in a supernatural Being is regarded as superstition. They claim that Buddhism is free from dogmatism.[26]

There is "no supreme law giver who rules and commands in the realm of the moral world."[27] God is not postulated. There are therefore also no bonds. Indeed, any bonds must be broken if man is to find himself.

For this no teaching is so well suited as that of Buddha, the enlightened, because it immediately shatters these concepts, knows no dogma, sets up no statements of faith, but in its own unique fashion allows everything to develop out of the depth of things, out of the nature of man.[28]

Naturally, there is also faith here. Schmidt seeks to prove that.

[24] Walter Holsten, "Buddhism in Germany," IRM, XLVIII (1959), 409.
[25] Ibid., p. 411.
[26] U Hla Bu, "The Christian Encounter with Buddhism in Burma," IRM, XLVII (1958), 174.
[27] Max Ladner, "Buddhistische Moral," Einsicht, 1956, p. 139.
[28] Schmidt, op. cit., p. 2.

This faith is not bound to the supernatural, however, but has grown out of man.

The trust, the faith that comes out of self-knowledge, is no longer related to something else. It is the faith which arises and grows from experimentation with one's self, which from the gradual penetration into one's own processes of life wins the certainty that only in ourselves the light shines beyond all dogma and statements of faith.[29]

Therefore content cannot be given to this faith from the outside. It arises through meditation, through determining "I am this" and "I am not that." Naturally, by this "I" is understood, not the personal individuality, but the supra-personal given quality in us, the metaphysical self. A transcendent "I" is understood.

The longer and the more intensively one examines the course of events in and around us, the more clearly one comes to the realization that they are transient and empty and without substance, in a word, that they are suffering. If the Hindu meditation is to be brought into a formula, "I am this," the formula for the meditation which Buddha has taught us would be, "I am not that; that doesn't belong to me; that is not my self."[30]

Thus every individuality—every being in the transcendent sense—is denied and thereby man remains the center of contemplation. It is a question of denying man's own existence. That really appears to be unnatural. In no religion, however, is man taken more seriously than in Buddhism, where all thought must concern itself with this "appearance of reality." The Buddhists themselves understand clearly that their analysis of existence cannot be proved. Their pronouncements are to be understood as working hypotheses. Man must meditate upon himself and discover what reality is. There is nothing alongside man which has permanence and stability. Therefore he goes into nirvana completely alone.

Although the Buddhist may deny the existence of everything, he would never doubt that there is at work in this world an incomprehensible something from which the Buddhist dharma

[29] *Ibid.*, p. 5.
[30] F. Kaufmann, "Die Welt ist Leiden," *Einsicht,* 1956, p. 44.

continuously emanates. "Dharma as such has no history. Only the external circumstances under which it works are subject to change."[31] This dharma, i.e., the teaching of non-existence, of suffering and of the end of suffering, is without beginning and without end. It constitutes itself once in each age in a Buddha who has progressed higher in his knowledge from existence to existence and who before his entry into nirvana reveals the dharma to mankind.

It is significant that this teaching is placed above the Christian idea of God.

> The divine in the purest and deepest sense is thus the unknowable principle of existence of the world, which is the self of us and of all things.[32]

> Buddha's teaching of a godless absolute as a super-personal spiritual foundation is perhaps nearer to the vital god-concept than the anthropomorphic concept of God that so many Christians make for themselves . . . Only when we have rediscovered the silent, infathomably profound, basis of existence, can we see the light kindle which appears in the creative life-principle (which we call Christ) emanating from the eternal First Cause.[33]

Here Christ must allow himself to be misused in order to prove Buddhism.

The God-relation is much more complicated in Hinduism.

> The principal thesis of the Vedanta teaches the absolute, unchangeable and simply indivisible uniformity of existence . . . [There is only] one thing, without a second one—that is reality, Brahma, the ultimate principle of substance.[34]

This concept of God thus derives from the idea that there is an eternal, unique, all determining power, and no empirical being

---

[31] Edward Conze, op. cit., p. 12.

[32] George Grimm, Das Glück, die Botschaft des Buddha (? 1933), p. 42.

[33] Hellmut von Schweinitz, Buddhismus und Christentum ("Glauben und Wissen," Nr. 14 [Munich: Ernst Reinhardt, 1955]), p. 47.

[34] Carl Keller, "The Vedanta Philosophy and the Message of Christ," IRM, XLII (1953), 378–379.

in addition. All empirical being is subject to development and decay. Man can therefore find his true existence only in this one being. Within Hinduism, the ways to it are various, but all ways can be traced to two basic points of reference. Historically, the chasm between this absolute and the empiric man could be traversed either by Yoga, through the painstaking training in the divine and thus along the way of knowledge and works: or the unification had to derive from the absolute itself and complete itself in mysticism. Both led to the result that the Indian became turned from the world because he wanted to flee the world of apparent reality. According to the newer Indian understanding, however, this position was basically false, for in both systems the divine was regarded as an opposite.

Today the pantheistic interpretation is espoused, that the divine is already in everything; as a result it is a question of man's making himself available to the divine for forming the world. Even the many gods of India are only a mode of expression of this one absolute. As a result one may not speak of a polytheism, but only of the one divinity which works in everything:

In this context is also to be found the uniquely Hindu concept according to which each god, no matter how low he otherwise may stand in the hierarchy, in the moment of worship becomes the one supreme god, who unites in himself all other gods by simultaneously becoming them.[35]

The one divinity is thus present in all things and all powers. It does not work mechanically. Therefore each person finds his own individuality in this divinity.

The divine penetrates his self, wells up and flows through him, absorbing him and enriching him within it. God is not for him another self, He is the real self closer than his own ego . . . In the order of nature, he keeps up his separate individuality; in the order of spirit, the divine has taken hold of him, remoulding his personality.[36]

---

[35] Herbert, *op. cit.*, p. 57.
[36] Radhakrishnan, *op. cit.*, p. 32. Cf. Friso Melzer, *Indische Weisheit und christliche Erkenntnis* (Tübingen: O. Reichl, 1948).

This teaching can naturally degenerate as with Vivekananda, who wanted only to rest in this self, while his master, Ramakrishna, was clear that man in this world cannot free himself from this world and from his ego. As a result he can only allow himself to be influenced by the divine, but he cannot become divine. "According to his nature God is eternity, purity and consciousness. Through his consciousness one becomes aware of all things. Man does not lose his own consciousness if he is obsessed with God."[37] Ramakrishna even knows that in the last analysis man cannot come to God. Even the longing for God is brought about by God. "The searching is being sought and the finding is being found; the way to God from man is in truth the way from God to man."[38]

In this transformed piety, God is understood as love. He wants to work upon the world. Aurobindo with his new practice of Yoga goes beyond this mysticism. He emphasizes the contrast to the divine more strongly. The chasm between the eternal spirit and the world can be bridged in that man through his spirit participates in God, the super-person, by which he becomes completely transformed. The more his spirit becomes united with the eternal spirit, the more the divine becomes the actual ego of the person. Here the supernatural element in man's nature is not directly assumed. It must be achieved. The Englishman, Brunton, has developed this Yoga further, so that the person himself becomes a super-person. Contrary to this Radhakrishnan feels that only mysticism is the solution to the question of God: God and the world constitute the one reality. Transcendent self and earthly self become a unity. Brunton points to the insufficiency of mysticism. It may be a resistance to orthodox beliefs, based on aversion to the forms and the hypocrisy in religion; in the last analysis, it leaves man unsatisfied because he does not find his true self in it and after each period of ecstasy there is a return to sobriety.[39]

Basically, the Indic understanding of God in all its variations is again nothing but a salvaging of the self-glorification of man.

[37] Wolff, *op. cit.*, p. 36.   [38] *Ibid.*, p. 40.   [39] Brunton, *op. cit.*, pp. 70–83.

It is distinguished from Buddhism only in that Buddhism radically eliminates the divine, while Hinduism seeks to establish the unity between God and man. Both religions appeal to man today because they grant him the right to determine for himself what is divine without having his own authority challenged.

In Islam things are quite different. Mohammed placed God transcendentally in the absolute so that he cannot be reached by man. Nevertheless there arose a strong mystic tendency in Islam. God is so presented, however, that man has only the choice of recognizing him or rejecting him. To be sure, Islam could not skirt the many philosophical difficulties, for it tries to assert the independence of man alongside this absolute god. It could only solve the problem thus: In the last analysis God does everything; man, however, through his free will adapts himself to God's intentions. God exists of and for himself. As the absolute master, he is also the master of mankind and determines their fate. Therefore he has announced his binding will to men in the Koran.

According to the teaching of the Ahmadiyya, God does not confront men with insoluble problems. For example, he performs no miracles which contradict natural laws. He respects the rationality of his creatures. No one can raise the question of justice in relation to God, for God is not bound by justice as man understands it. He does only good to mankind. The Ahmadiyya does not even mention the problem of predestination which plays such a large part in Islam. Man must surrender himself to God for better or worse. In Islam that is the one possible position.

God is [in judgment] not bound to human standards. When he passes judgment, he will take the right of no one into consideration, but it is completely up to him to demand what is required of man or to absolve him from it.[40]

The propitiatory sacrifice is thus an offense to God, a questioning of his existence as God.

[40] *Der Heilige Quran*, p. 143.

If these laws prescribe a punishment, then God determines the punishment. On the other hand, God has made known laws by means of which his characteristics of mercy and forgiveness have found expression. If these laws call for mercy and forgiveness, then these characteristics come into play.[41]

In no other religion does God have so little relation to man as in Islam. There is no tie between him and men. Nevertheless, there is a point in the Koran which speaks to contemporary men. God remains the Lord, and man is delivered up to Him, but man is not directed to His mercy through a savior. If man keeps the prescriptions of this God, he can assure himself that God will reward him for it according to His laws. Thus everything here rests upon the conduct of man. He can achieve blessedness for himself. About this there is no doubt. Man remains the free man, even though he has to enslave himself.

4. THE OTHER ETHIC

The intention of the three religions is alike in one thing: Man is a free personality and cannot be called to account by the divine. Nowhere in these religions is there a concern that man by his nature is a sinner. If he has the right understanding of existence, he is free and can save himself. Therefore the way is shown to him in religion. Thus he need confront no decision of conscience as to how he shall relate himself to the divine. A decision of the will is enough, and with it his obedience becomes a one-time, but self-perpetuating, act. Only in Islam is the divine law prescribed for him. In the other two religions, man has the possibility of finding the right way himself through meditation. The good is then always that which helps him toward inner freedom even when it is most strongly bound to asceticism.

Buddhism proceeds from the thesis: "The madness of ego is precisely a symptom of the condition of illness in which man finds himself."[42] Man must become free of it. He can free himself from ego by freeing himself from his ignorance. Through right knowl-

---

[41] *Ibid.*, p. 149.
[42] Gustav Mensching, *Gut und Böse im Glauben der Völker* (2d rev. ed.; Stuttgart: E. Klotz, 1950), p. 53.

edge he will be led to salvation. "The fundamental object was to *get free*—free from all undesirable conditions and mental objects, free also from more desirable ones."[43] This freedom, in the last analysis, is the goal of salvation.

The Buddhist does not mean freedom to be master of man, not unrestrained freedom, but freedom to do good. Good, however, is just as little capable of being defined as is ultimate truth. The good encompasses everything that is circumscribed by the eight-fold path. "It is certainly a fact that in Buddhism that is 'good' which leads toward nirvana and that is 'not good' which leads away from it."[44]

Thus the good is everything which frees man from his self-seeking will so that without passions, without envy, uninfluenced by anything and elevated above the things of life, he can complete his time on earth. He may in no case add to suffering. Since every cause of suffering is seen in the eagerness of life, he must seek to fight his passions and to overcome by renunciation:

Knowing that no god and no church, neither ceremonies nor priests can help him or protect him, the Buddhist sees himself necessarily constrained to rely on his own efforts and thus gains faith in himself. No one can deny that the feeling of dependence on God or another imaginary power must necessarily weaken man's belief in his own strength and his own responsibility, while on the other hand through trust in his own power his self-reliance is given foundation and strength.[45]

Man must then believe in himself; that is the key to the Buddhist ethic. This is not meant, however, in the sense of idealism, where it is taught that man can also discover the moral precepts himself, but man is called to self-reliance in order to pursue Buddha's path of salvation.

This path, it is claimed, gives him not only guidance, but also strength:

[43] Edward Conze, *et al.* (trans. and ed.), *Buddhist Texts Through the Ages* (New York: Philosophical Library, 1957), p. 11.
[44] Ladner, *op. cit.*, p. 143.
[45] Nyanatiloka, "Über die Beeinflussung eines Volkes durch den Buddhismus," *Einsicht*, 1956, p. 56.

It is impossible to come into close contact with this teaching without being spurred into action by it. The primary feature of the teaching of Buddhism is its power to change the disposition of man. It makes the cruel sympathetic, the hostile friendly, the hardhearted mild, the superficial deep, the ignorant wise, the lazy ambitious, the selfish selfless.[46]

The goal is to lead men to the all-encompassing good. Resentment and hate are to be overcome by meditation. Good belongs to all forms of life. They shall all become happy. Happiness is the actual goal of salvation and the ethic becomes here the point of departure for salvation.

"But always the Buddhist love is the same to all creatures and that comprises its greatness. It does not confine itself to this life, but sees its point of departure in another earthly life (indeed in many others) which precedes this incarnation."[47] The good must refrain from all force, for force is always an expression of bondage to self. Hence the weak is protected from the strong. Therefore there can be no wars in Buddhist countries. It is also forbidden to Buddhist missionaries to preach animosity and hate against non-Buddhists. This man cannot do out of hand. He must prepare himself for it daily through meditation and must daily practice it. This all-encompassing good "follows from the understanding that all living creatures, from man down to the worm, are subject to the same laws and conditions of life. As I am, so are they; as they are, so am I."[48]

In order to reach this inner attitude, the men in Thailand participate in exercises in the monasteries, which even the king does not shirk. Once one has gained the right attitude, the questions of life are no longer a problem. It becomes easy for him to keep the commandments and to find the right attitude to his body. It is significant that the Buddhists practice no asceticism which is not determined by this basic attitude. This holds only, it is noted, of the seeking and struggling man. The people concern them-

[46] Soma Thera, op. cit., p. 77.
[47] von Schweinitz, op. cit., p. 48.
[48] Nyanatiloka, op. cit., p. 56.

selves little about this inner preparation. They prefer even today
to build pagodas and trust in good works instead of participating
in this inner effort.

The Hindu ethic is chiefly given in the many prescriptions of
the Hindu religion, but among the mystics the deed is called forth
by the divine. Since the divine is understood only as the good,
men should also do only good, i.e., open themselves to the divine
so that the good may be done.

The truth of human existence is the love of God. In it man lives his
profound destiny; he experiences his highest fulfillment; he performs
his greatest service; in it he becomes himself . . . In it man comes to
the truth of himself because it raises him above all his own impotence.[49]

The love of God also orders the relation of man to his surrounding world. Radhakrishnan desires a somewhat altered way in
mysticism. Man has seen

that at rock bottom things are good, and that there is a power which
is ceaselessly overcoming evil and transforming it into good . . . He
has the sense of power by which he creates meaning and beauty out
of the conflicts of human desires and passions . . . The saved one
becomes an elemental force of nature, a dynamo of spirit, working at
a stupendously high velocity. The renunciation he has practised does
not require him to flee from the world of works, but only to slay the
ego sense.[50]

All Hindus agree that non-violence is the goal of practical
action. This is not, however, to be equated with the goodness of
Buddha. While the Buddhist is elevated above all quarreling,
non-violence is a program for the protection of men. Therefore
non-violence is not to be equated with cowardice. Gandhi could
even have recourse to violence when India's freedom demanded
it. He required, however, that men always hold to the truth. That
is only possible, however, if a man recognizes his errors. Gandhi
teaches, therefore, that there is no purification of the heart without recognition of guilt.

Here it would be worthwhile to say a word about Yoga, which

[49] Wolff, *op. cit.*, p. 49.   [50] Radhakrishnan, *op. cit.*, pp. 52–53.

still plays a significant role in the Indian ethic. Almost all Indians, even Radhakrishnan, believe they cannot dispense with asceticism, since man must be led to selflessness. Asceticism is the means of healing the total personality. The more strongly the mystic tendency is emphasized, the more asceticism must become the means for the ethic, "through which one strives for quieting of the passions and dissolution of the personal structure in the life of the soul."[51] In asceticism Yoga, especially in its lower degrees, is of great importance, because it gives men practice in self-denial. In the higher degrees, it serves exclusively for the training of the spirit in order to find unity with the divine. Yoga tries to make men capable of good, but many Indians misuse it and thereby deceive others. Brunton used Yoga in order to arrive at his philosophy of the "Overself," which teaches how to unite the spirit with the all-spirit in the consciousness. The way, to be sure, is so difficult that it can scarcely find followers.

The ethic of Islam has many external similarities with the Buddhist ethic even though they are basically completely different. The Moslem, too, acts according to prescription as does the Buddhist. However, while in Buddhism everything is directed toward overcoming the self, in Islam everything depends on obedience to the cultic prescriptions which are supposed to be a means of help toward "surrender" to God. For the Moslem, the law in its moral, social, and cultic demands is a unit. The more man practices it, the more he finds his spiritual abilities and ascends from virtue to virtue.

In the sphere of moral law the Quran establishes the principle that the higher moral characteristics develop from the appropriate use of natural abilities. Man should not allow his natural abilities be suppressed and disturbed, just as he should also not subject himself to their absolute mastery.[52]

So that the natural characteristics do not gain mastery, the Moslem has to fulfill cultic prescriptions. Regular prayer, fasting, etc. are his great aids. They will help him to a true brotherhood,

[51] Mensching, op. cit., p. 30.   [52] Der Heilige Quran, p. 155.

for in Islam all believers have equal rights. The poor must be cared for. There are no racial differences. The Ahmadiyya even insists that in Islam slavery is forbidden. One can only say such a thing if one regards the whole world as stupid. The most pertinent judgment over the ethic of Islam was given by Mensching:

The divinity of the will sets up demands without the religion itself offering help toward their fulfillment.[53]

Even in the ethic, man is encouraged to reach his goals himself. All the religions claim to be only a way to this goal. Ethical behavior in these religions does not serve the good itself, but is always a preliminary stage of salvation. Therefore the ethic of these religions cannot be separated from the self-centered goal of man's salvation.

5. THE WAY OF SALVATION

We have already established how radically different from the Gospel is man's understanding of self in these religions, and hence the understanding of God. As a result the way of salvation must also be completely different. If the ultimate goal of salvation through Jesus Christ is man's finding the way back to the right communion with God, then this goal is not at all striven for in Buddhism. In Hinduism it is assumed to exist already. In Islam this communion does not exist at all; here there is only a community of men which Allah establishes. In Buddhism and Hinduism, man must become free of his imagined self so that he can find true existence in the divine. In Islam, the transiency of men is nullified by the transfer into Paradise. Nowhere, however, shall man be freed of sin and evil; rather, he can achieve his salvation for himself because he is considered basically good.

The English Buddhist, Humphreys, asks for Buddhism: Who is saved? To which he gives the answer: "The ephemeral self must die, so much is clear; but what shall achieve salvation, become enlightened, reach Nirvana, when this unreal, separative, misery-causing self is dead? The answer is man."[54] It is thus

---

[53] Mensching, op. cit., p. 124.   [54] Humphreys, op. cit., p. 13.

man, or let us say true man, man raised above apparent reality. He is saved. It is a salvation into humanity, out of the false existence into the one existence which can exist according to the Indic conception.

If we pose the further question: Who saves? we receive the shocking answer: No one! "Even Buddhas do but point the way, and the individual must sooner or later work out his own salvation with diligence."[55] Buddha only shows the way. He is the savior insofar as he shows men the way of salvation. He claims absolute validity for this way.

It is different in northern Buddhism, where Buddha became the savior. The deed of Buddha is so great that it surpasses the redemptive death of Christ. This assertion is to be found again and again. Jesus was not free of anger and violence; Buddha on the contrary was perfect benevolence.[56] Jesus' death on the cross is, to be sure, perfect selflessness and self-sacrifice in the service of mankind:

Buddha, too, succeeded in a similar act of selflessness when after his enlightenment he renounced the peace of nirvana and for fifty years took upon himself a wearisome journeying, preaching and teaching in order to show the way to overcome suffering to those "whose eyes are scarcely covered with dust" and to demonstrate practically in the example of his own life. His death was, to be sure, a death into beauty and perfect peace, but nonetheless the success of his teaching and of his personal example was no less than that of Jesus of Nazareth.[57]

Here there are no concepts such as sin and grace because there is no God against whom man can sin and who needs to grant grace. As a result there is also no mediator who must reconcile men with God. The important thing is not the savior, but the path of salvation. "No one could show the path as he [Buddha] could. Not to have found the truth of suffering, its source and remission, but to have found the path which leads out of the insanity of the 'I' and of 'mine' which brings about suffering is Buddha's unique

[55] *Ibid.*, p. 61.
[56] Otto Wolff, "Wandlung des Christusbildes im modernen Hinduismus," *EMZ*, 1956, p. 103.   [57] Ladner, *op. cit.*, p. 141.

and saving act."[58] Whoever follows this path is saved. He stands beyond good and evil; nothing more can disturb him spiritually. It is thus "a teaching without Christ and without grace, but with Buddha and the act of the self. It certainly finds a willing ear among many in the dechristianized West."[59]

What is the goal of salvation? It is said to be nirvana. We know how difficult it is to give meaning to this concept. Today it is generally considered to be one way of life which is absolute fulfillment:

Nirvana is a condition which cannot at all be presented intellectually. Because the perfection in nirvana is unfathomable, being or not being have no relationship to it.

Nirvana is a condition which has no points of relationship with the earthly side of human existence. It is conclusive departure from the cycle of birth, the cessation of everything that we understand as our existence, neither space nor time, neither inner nor outer being, neither existence nor non-existence, simply the unchangeable, the eternal, which has neither beginning nor end, for all suffering ceases.[60]

If that is so, then we must ask ourselves, to be sure, whether nirvana is simply a fiction or whether there lies behind it simply the desire for happiness which one cannot conceive in a life bound by creation. If I know nothing of nirvana and it has no point of relationship to human existence, can it then be salvation? In the context of Buddhism, man can only ascertain what he is not, rather than what he is. Does it then make any sense to speak of salvation?

The goal of salvation in Hinduism is similar. Man shall come out of the wheel of rebirth and be translated into actual existence. This is here understood as the divine. If formerly the way of salvation was asceticism, today it is primarily mysticism as represented by Radhakrishnan:

It is the ego sense, the illusion, that each of us is an exclusive unity

[58] Schmidt, op. cit., p. 6.
[59] Thomas B. W. Gramberg, "Ceylon auf dem Hintergrund des Buddhismus," Evangelisches Missionsmagazin (hereafter referred to as EMM), 1957, p. 69.   [60] von Schweinitz, op. cit., pp. 35–36.

sharply marked off from whatever lies outside his body in space and beyond his experience in time. So long as the illusion of a separate ego persists, existence in the temporal process is inevitable . . . The abandonment of the ego is the identification with a fuller life and consciousness. The soul is raised to a sense of its universality . . . The secret of the Cross is the crucifixion of the ego and the yielding to the will of God.[61]

The meaning of salvation is thus that man becomes one with his true being which lies enclosed in the universal existence. With this, great emphasis is laid today upon simultaneous world affirmation. This is supposed to be brought out above all by asceticism. Man shall do good for his own sake and thus lead the world to good. Thereby daily life is placed at the service of the divine. If man allows himself at the same time to be filled with the divine, then he presses forward upon the way of mysticism toward the universal self. He can then even (according to Brunton) become such a unity with the universal self that he becomes the "Overself."

Brunton names seven characteristics of philosophy which should lead to this goal:[62] (1) It seeks the truth above all. (2) It hopefully preserves and does not give up before the goal is reached. (3) It is gained by learning to think correctly and not by accepting the traditional opinions; it distinguishes between the ephemeral and the eternal. (4) The individual must cultivate inner detachment from the affairs of life. (5) He must have concentration, calmness, and reverie—which are the basis of the art of meditation. (6) He must discipline his feelings and purify the character by rationally controlling his emotions, for feelings such as hate and greed as well as evil deeds keep him from the goal. (7) He must give up his ego, i.e., listen, evaluate critically, and seek after the truth without concern for his previous opinions.

When we look over this way of salvation, which is no easier

[61] Radhakrishnan, *op. cit.*, p. 97. Cf Friso Melzer, *Christus und die indischen Erlösungswege* (Tübingen: O. Reichl, 1949).
[62] Brunton, *op. cit.*, pp. 118–142.

in the Indic systems, we are struck by the great exertion with which man must save himself. Hinduism and Buddhism do not question whether man can actually do that. They do not consider the many men who are incapable of such speculation. The primary question remains whether there is any possibility of salvation emanating from man. Both see salvation in the discovery of the actual self which is subject to no decay. Man would like to have the certainty of being something. Is that not, however, the ultimate and deepest bondage to self? What if man cannot follow this way of salvation? Then he remains in his misery and must wait until in some existence or other he finds the possibility to do so. Under no circumstances do such religions offer a consolation to men nor do they offer any certainty of salvation. This is only offered where God works salvation. That, however, happened in Jesus Christ.

The Ahmadiyya immediately presents a series of reproaches against Jesus. He thought always only of Israel and designated other men as swine and dogs. How could he be God's son when he curses? How much more noble Mohammed appears than Christ! Furthermore there is no need for a savior for when man repents and does good he achieves Paradise. On the other hand, the Ahmadiyya sect offers men a tangible teaching of salvation, which to be sure does not depart from the Koran, but which is not as conspicuously embellished as with Mohammed. Through the Koran, man is preserved in faith and led to good works. There are three stages of blessedness which man can achieve. They are distributed in judgment according to the deeds of men: (1) complete blessedness which can already be earned here; (2) incomplete blessedness, in which man still has the opportunity to earn complete blessedness in the beyond; and (3) suspended blessedness, in which man must first pay the penalty of his punishment in purgatory before he can enter into perfect blessedness. Perdition is thus only a transitional condition. It will become meaningless when all the souls of men are refined. Death is only a passing over of man into another world. Ahmad is proclaimed as the universal savior. He stands under the divine call, brings the one authorized explanation of revelation, and is therefore the only one who can show men the way to salvation.

The Bahai sect, on the other hand, extols Bab, i.e., the door of the knowledge of God, as the savior. This sect wants to realize salvation in this world. This world of darkness is juxtaposed to a world of light in which all social problems are solved. A realm of peace is instituted. In this realm, supposedly, men can partake of all joys.

6. THE UNITY OF MANKIND

Today the three world religions are bursting their territorial limits and want to win world recognition. They lay claim to all of mankind, not only in reaction to the Christian world mission, but also in the knowledge that today mankind has become united in its economic, social, and spiritual distress. Therefore it is regarded as a unity by the religions. To recognize it as a unity means, however, to become aware of the deep yearning for peace, to sense the fateful bondage under the idea of power. Should we wonder that today, out of an awareness of their mission, all religions seek to offer help to man? Hinduism and Buddhism must do that from inner duty because, according to the teaching of transmigration of the soul, Asiatic men in their future existence can be born into other peoples. In addition to this it happens that for both religions the solution of social problems has become a question of the fate of their peoples. The distress is so great that today in the area of both these religions sects and pseudo-religions offer themselves and promise help. That is especially the case in the Buddhist territory where the sects seek to perfect themselves by means of Christianity.

Taking everything into consideration, Buddhism especially is aware that it is acquiring a significant influence over the spiritual life of men. Humphreys believes he can prove that Western science is fast approaching the Buddhist explanation of the world and is today making discoveries which Buddha has already announced. Besides this, one can follow up precisely how much the Western intellectuals take over from Buddhism, thereby strengthening its influence. Similarly Hellmuth Hecker states: "The Western man wants no new belief; he wants knowledge which will stand up against reasonable thought. The critical European does not want the husk of Buddhism, but the kernel."[63] Buddhism is concerned above all with bringing peace to all mankind. That is not possible when one seeks to influence only separate peoples.

In Hinduism, it was Ramakrishna more than anyone else who announced the brotherhood of man and began to set it in practice among the outcastes in India. His ideas were taken up by Gandhi, who addressed himself to all mankind with his program of non-violence. We know how fascinating this message is whenever it is again announced by Nehru in times of political crisis. The Asiatics today know better than Western men that a future war would be a question of existence or non-existence. Radhakrishnan has drawn the strongest conclusions from this teaching: "To say that there is only one God is to affirm that there is only one community of mankind . . . The feeling of fellowship with the whole of humanity is implanted in our nature. We are members of a world community."[64] Therefore he also seeks ways toward the great human community. He believes that the religions have the duty to make the whole world one. They should not be means of separation, but ways of unity. At the world conference of the religions in 1957 he said: "If this conference causes you to respect the other religions and the other men and brings you the awareness that there are no chosen races, no chosen peoples, and no preferred men, but that each has the possibility within himself to grow into the divine, it will have achieved something great."

In Islam, the view which took its orientation from faith in God was always directed toward mankind as a whole. The Moslems live in the belief that all mankind belongs to Allah. Both the sects previously named strongly emphasize this idea. The goal of the Ahmadiyya sect is to raise mankind socially and to estab-

[63] Hellmuth Hecker, "Der Buddhismus und das Abendland," *Einsicht*, 1957, p. 70.   [64] Radhakrishnan, *op. cit.*, pp. vii–viii, 40.

lish the peace of the world.[65] The Bahai sect announces: All mankind must be regarded as a unity; all men should independently investigate the truth and come to peace.

These religions know that the question of humanity today can be solved only on a global basis. They consciously commit themselves to peace. That makes an impression on men. Up until now the West has developed no program for peace.

7. THE UNITY OF THE RELIGIONS

Men are faced today with universal problems. They therefore expect a common and universal solution. They feel everything which separates is disturbing, not only political passions, but also the ideological blocs which divide mankind. They also view the opposing positions of the religions as disturbing factors. Therefore the religions today either seek to establish unity through missionary work, or they suggest a uniting and working together. What is occurring today in the Christian ecumenical movement finds a parallel in the other religions. The separate religions first find points held in common within themselves. In addition there are attempts to unite the religions in an active program of help in view of humanity's suffering under the anxiety of the world. Just as the ecumenical movement was supported theologically only after its inception, so only now are considerations being raised in the religions as to whether such unions are possible based on the inner comprehension of the religions. No religion wants to surrender itself in this process. A common denominator is therefore sought. This has been found in the principle of the equality of all religions.

The assertion of the equality of religions is actually an essential element in many religions. Mohammed, for example, set up the principle that God has revealed himself to every people, in this way all peoples have received a part in the revelation of God, and thus there exists a common basis for all religions. We know that even Christians make the attempt again and again to prove

[65] Emmanuel Kellerhals, *Der Islam: Seine Geschichte, seine Lehre, sein Wesen* (2d ed.; Basel: Baseler Missionsbuchhandlung, 1956), p. 275.

"original monotheism." The statement is often repeated that basically all religions say the same thing, the differences coming only from the fact that each religion realized itself in historical forms.[66] From this is usually drawn the false conclusion that those religions which have least bound themselves in dogma stand closest to the original and form the basis for the other religions —Hinduism and Buddhism, especially claim this for themselves. All religions would share in one another. The single awareness of God would be their content. All religions represent the same truth.

To crystallize this, many analogies are used in the literature today: All clocks go according to the sun, but no clock is exact. Each religion is such a clock, but only the sun, God himself, gives the correct time.—Truth is like a pond. The water is always the same, but men bathe in different places. The one travels upon the water in a boat, the other in a ship, another upon a raft. —Truth is like food which is prepared in different ways. —A much used picture is the elephant described by blind men. Each feels only a part, but never understands the whole. —Religion is a matter of taste. We know the description by Gandhi, who compared the religions with a flower garden. Each flower has a different color, a different odor, but they are all flowers and they all stand in the same garden. —Ramakrishna compared the religions to different colors.

All these comparisons suggest that it is not religions that are absolute, but man, who has the right to choose for himself the religion which best suits him. He is not bound to the absolute, but he himself is the master. One does not ask whether God determines what truth is, but only how man can recognize the truth.

Others say again, all religions are alike in that they have the same goal. They are supposed to improve man, train him, bring out the good in him. U Nu goes so far as to say they have the task of taming the wild beast in man. Salvation seems here to

---

[66] Thomas Ohm, *Asia Looks at Western Christianity*, trans. Irene Marinoff (Edinburgh and London: Nelson, 1959), p. 32.

be a by-product.[67] Against the thesis of the equality of all religions, the Indian theologian David G. Moses turns very sharply.
He first points to the actual differences and then continues:

> But not all paths which we wander are His. Some of them are essen-
> tially paths of man's own wilful making, paths cut out by his insensate
> ambition, insatiable cupidity and avaricious greed. There are paths
> that lead away from God, just as there are paths which lead to Him.
> Not all ways are exactly the same. Some ways are blind alleys and
> lead nowhere. It is not true to say that, whatever the way, it leads
> ultimately to the heavenly city.[68]

This position must of necessity devalue all religions of revelation, and designate them as overbearing, unrealistic, backward
and difficult. This reproach is made especially against Christianity and Islam, but the latter is only opposed where it runs
counter to the other religions, while with the help of Islam the
religions march forward against Christianity on a broad front.
Here we can establish two lines. On the one hand the attempt is
made to affirm that all religions stem from the same root. That
is very easy to prove, for instance, on the part of Hinduism in
relation to Buddhism, for Buddhism actually did proceed from
Hinduism. The Indic people prove with great satisfaction, therefore, that Buddhism is more and more like Hinduism. It is also
not difficult to prove as concerns Islam that it is a corrupt
deviation from Christianity. It is difficult, however, to verify
the direct dependence of biblical revelation upon India. Against
this stands, in addition, the essential understanding of revelation in which everything is thought to proceed from God, while
in India it is always thought to proceed from man.

Buddhism has the easiest task here, for between it and Christianity there are a number of parallels.

(It should certainly not be overlooked that in parallel practices
Buddhism expresses something quite different from the Gospel!)

[67] U Hla Bu, *op. cit.*, p. 175.
[68] David G. Moses, "Christianity and the Non-Christian Religions," *IRM*,
XLIII (1954), 150.

Since Buddhism is the older religion, it is believed that Jesus was dependent upon Buddha:

As Jesus in Palestine announced the liberating doctrine of over-coming the world and of religious inwardness over against the narrow worldliness of Judaism with its anthropomorphic folkgod, this event also passed in principle and consequence into the process of the encounter between Hellas and India. Whether the influence of India upon Christ has been more direct or indirect may remain undecided.[69]

It is pointed out how from the beginning the church had to come to grips with the influences of Buddhism. This fact is not to be denied. Precisely that, however, proves that the church would not let the Gospel be pulled into the undertow of the Indic religions, but knew that it was something independent. Therefore it set itself against these influences, because on the basis of the Gospel it was precisely these influences that it had to overcome.

Von Schweinitz presents much material in support of the similarity between Christianity and Buddhism.[70] Buddhism already existed in the Near East at the time of Jesus. Agreements in the traditions are undeniably present. Buddha and Jesus belonged to the same brotherhood. "We are interested in the logic of religious experience, and Buddha as well as Jesus is a notable witness of it." Even the evangelists were influenced by the cult of Buddha. In addition, Buddhism and Catholicism have many practices in common: celibacy, confession, veneration of relics, rosary, tonsure, bells, altar rites, incense, flowers, lights, and song. The question even arises whether in the thirty years of which we know nothing, Jesus was not himself in India. Above all von Schweinitz sees a common ground in the fig tree motif. For him the Nathaniel episode is proof that Jesus must have belonged to the Essenes. He comes to the conclusion that Christianity as Jesus understood it was Buddhism fulfilled, and Buddhism was Christianity fulfilled. The claim of Christianity to being absolute persists without basis. As a result there can only

[69] Hecker, *op. cit.*, p. 67.   [70] von Schweinitz, *op. cit.*, pp. 50 ff.

be co-operation. Does von Schweinitz really not see that in word and deed Jesus was completely dependent on God and placed himself completely on the foundation of the Old Testament? These two facts separate him as sharply from Buddha as fire is separated from water.

There are no such parallels between Hinduism and Christianity. If one ignores the Krishna legend, there are scarcely any points of comparison. Therefore the Hindus proceed from the statement that there can be only one God and as a result the Indic God is the same as the Christian God. Radhakrishnan, especially, using all contemporary sources and the history of Christian dogma, attempts to show proof that though Christianity does not depend directly upon India, India has continuously influenced the thought of the theologians. Today he sees hope in the fact that even in Christianity the spirit is becoming more and more the source of knowledge.

An attempt is made, especially on the part of Islam, to present Christianity as a backward, out-of-date religion. Since Islam is itself derivative, it cannot argue in the same manner as the Indic religions. It is here even under attack, inasmuch as the Indic religions accuse it of having hindered the fusion of Indic thought with Christianity, lying as it does as a great barricade between India and the West. Therefore Islam replies that, as the last religion to come into being, she must have the best revelation. The Quran states first that all the names for God among the various peoples always designate the same God. "God is one, as the law to which the world is subject, as the ordering principle which holds the world together, is one."[71] All religions have the same God, therefore religion must be a means to union. Since it is impossible for Islam to recognize other religions, it seeks the unity through itself. In this it proceeds from revelation: Every people has had its revelation but none has been complete. Only when humanity was on the way toward unity did Allah give the Koran and thus the final and complete revela-

[71] *Der Heilige Quran*, p. 18.

tion. Therefore all religions are preliminary stages toward Islam; all find in it their completion and fulfillment.—The tendency toward arrogance is especially present in the sects. It is further said that Islam is the most modern religion. The conclusion is simple: If these conditions hold, there can be a unifying of the religions only through Islam.

Because of the Asiatic insistence on unity in the religions, Christianity in its present form meets with opposition. According to the Asiatics, man must break through the organized church and through the dogmas in order to find a unifying factor. Hinduism boasts that it has no dogmas. Buddhism says that only immature men quarrel. "Those who are uncertain do *not yet* quarrel; the noble disciples *no longer quarrel*. Only those Buddhists quarrel who are still in the process of becoming holy disciples."[72] From this viewpoint sharp reproaches are made against the intolerance of the Christian church and against its missionary work. It is pointed out that no blood has yet flowed for the spread of Buddhism. The statement does not hold true in this way, however. Even though there were no crusades in Buddhism, and it had no Inquisition, it has happened repeatedly in China's history that the political activity of Buddhism has abolished Christianity. Also the messianism which is widespread in Buddhist territory can lead to wars.

Hinduism today strives to become the reservoir for all religions. It carries out a process of amalgamation in India:

Hinduism recognizes that each religion is inextricably bound up in its culture and can grow organically. While it is aware that all religions have not attained to the same level of truth and goodness, it insists that they all have a right to express themselves. Religions reform themselves by interpretation and adjustment to one another. The Hindu attitude is one of positive fellowship, not negative tolerance. The different cults are brought into mutually helpful relations.[73]

The Parliament of the Religions, founded by Sivananda, also pursues this purpose.[74]

[72] Hellmuth Hecker, "Streitende Buddhisten," *Einsicht*, 1956, p. 135.
[73] Radhakrishnan, *op. cit.*, p. 335.   [74] Sastri, *op. cit.*, pp. 204–210.

When we ponder what has been said, it becomes surprisingly clear that the much used thesis of the equality of all religions, which among us is used as a basis for religious indifference, has the function of protection and confession in the non-Christian religions. Because all religions are equally justified, they also have the right to exist, the right to perfect and modernize themselves, and the right to spread themselves. A Christian cannot speak in this way because from the viewpoint of Christianity he cannot recognize these religions in their method of self-salvation; if he does recognize them, he immediately denies his Master. For the rest that statement is, for Western understanding, the most comfortable position one can take. It shows neither great acquaintance with the religions, nor critical thought.

5

The Challenge of the Religions

1. THE WORLD BECOMES "RELIGIOUS"

We are living in a time when men are turning in increasing numbers to religion. To date this process has scarcely been noticed by the church; it is taking place specifically in non-Christian areas. To date only a few Christian churches are profiting by this general development; e.g., the churches in North and South America, or those in Russia, Africa, and Korea. In the other areas, however, this development is taking place alongside the church. In East Asia and in part of Africa the sects are popping out of the ground like mushrooms. They are proof for the fact that men are engaged in a religious search and that they are finding no real answer in any religion. In our area the religious awakening expresses itself primarily in the most primitive forms of religion.

In Germany one is immediately struck by the especially strong spread of magic. This includes astrology. Even the "Christian" newspapers have astrological tables, and the readers evidently find nothing amiss in this. Both phenomena are a sign that contemporary man is no longer satisfied with the material security of his existence; he wants to have an inner assurance and therefore he turns again to the most primitive forms of religion. Men seek a security which carries no ethical duty with it. In this is also included the wide spread of Yoga literature which trains man to progress from the usual practice of relaxation to religious concentration. All this is a proof that contemporary man no longer sees any answer in the purely scientific explanation of events or in the Marxist explanation, and that he no longer finds any satisfaction in the purely technological perfection of life.

To this is added the appearance of new worship forms. Even the dechristianized man does not want to do without the identifying marks of the holy in his life. Even those who are estranged from the church require ceremonies of dedication. Life is to be brought into relation with the numinous so that man is armed against fate. The youth dedication in the area of communism and of atheism reflects similar concern. The world is becoming more religious; therefore, even the materialistic ideological movements can no longer afford to be non-religious.

No matter how much contemporary man through his striving for a higher standard of living has fallen prey to the search for pleasure, there nevertheless is also evident in mankind an ascetic quality from which even the church profits, but which also drives many men to the other religions. In order to recognize the real religious longing we must ask ourselves how contemporary man would act were the pleasure of the senses not continually aroused by business-oriented advertising, were his desires not whipped up and his yearnings increased by a conscienceless industry. A completely different man would appear.

In this development it is a question of a world-wide process. We ought to give these phenomena the greatest attention, for in them lies a certain promise for Christianity. The world is becoming more religious. That means, however, that materialism has today passed its peak, and will apparently disappear if it is not artificially maintained by the capitalism of industry on the one hand and by communism on the other hand. It is a fact, however, that materialism as well as atheism has emptied the soul of man so that today he is again seeking religious answers. No one can remain in a vacuum. It is a question of who is to fill this vacuum.

Because we as a church take no notice of these facts and seek no answers for these men, it is not clear to us how dangerous the offerings of the sects and the other religions are. When we speak of the challenge of the world religions, we must recognize this situation. We must not evaluate their missionary activity only according to the statistical figures, but we must see how through the activity of certain sects the ground is already prepared for these religions. In this presentation we can, of course, hold up only a few traits of these sects for attention without giving a manual of the sects.

2. THE CHRISTIAN FELLOWSHIP SECT

When we speak of this "fashionable sect of the educated," we must proceed from the question: Compared to the Gospel, what unique thing do they offer? It is the perfection of Christianity through theosophy, or better stated, through the anthroposophy of Steiner, which goes back to India. Its world concept, the mystic concept of the unity of the world, the teaching of karma, liberation from material bondage, ennobling of the material through the blood of Christ, indeed even the emphasis on the ethic as a means of salvation arise from India with theosophy as the intermediary.[1] Christianity had to be reinterpreted according to the wisdom of India. It was merged into Indic gnosticism. Even here man becomes the final measure of all things. He must save himself and actively help to tear himself more and more from materialization. Even the Indic understanding of religion is taken over.

Although the Christian Fellowship in its main teachings lets a discipline of secrecy prevail, it still does not demand that its followers should leave the church. It consciously wants to make it impossible to define the boundary separating it from the church. In this way it is more dangerous than sects which work

---

[1] Paul Huber, *Kirche und anthroposophisches Christentum: Eine kritische Einführung in das anthroposophische Weltbild unter besonderer Berücksichtigung der Christophie* (Zollikon: Evangelischer Verlag, 1957). See also H. W. Schomerus, *Die Anthroposophie Steiners und Indien* (Erlangen, 1922)

in the open. Thus the church is infiltrated unawares with Indic thought. In addition a strong influence is exercised by the Waldorf schools, which are among the best schools in Germany and are therefore attended by the children of the educated. These schools have overcome the purely secular school system and have integrated the teaching of anthroposophical principles into a total program of personality development such as one no longer finds today in the Christian private schools.

In this connection must also be mentioned theosophy, which today has become a world movement with two branches in Germany. There is the German Territorial Theosophical Society and the Theosophical Society, West German Section. The Theosophical Society has as its goal:

(1.) to build a core of the brotherhood of mankind without distinction of race, nation, faith, social status, or sex;

(2.) to encourage the comparative study of religion, philosophy, and science;

(3.) to search into the still unclarified natural laws and the powers of the soul which lie hidden within man.[2]

Through theosophy as well, Indic traditions have been carried among our people and made to bear fruit.

3. THE NEW THOUGHT MOVEMENT

The New Thought Movement, which next to the Christian Fellowship is probably the largest syncretistic group among Germans, has a great deal in common with Christian Science and with theosophy. It claims to offer a spiritually based world view which can be brought to bear upon the practical matters of life. It is related to the American New Thought Movement which teaches the eternity of the supreme, the holiness and finally the immortality of man, because he can, through the divine within himself, spiritually overcome illness and death. The followers seek a life of unending happiness, an eternal life beginning already here on earth. They believe this can be achieved through "new thoughts." A mysticism tending toward Buddhist medita-

[2] Kurt Hutten, *Materialdienst* (Stuttgart: Quellverlag, 1954), p. 140.

tion is espoused. In it there is also a place left for Jesus Christ, but he is only recognized as a model. They seek the essential point of all religions. One sees in this the Indic "I am." Here the concern is also for the problem of man's existence. Man would like to escape the transitory world in the very way that Buddha showed. The true self or being of man is intangible, is beyond all becoming and decay, the one thing that is certain for man. He will not disappear in death. The movement wants to transmit these Indic insights to others. In principle man can no longer be moved by any influences, not even by illness and pain, if he makes this insight his own. He is inwardly freed from everything. Within the German-language area the movement already has over 2000 groups with over 100,000 members.[3]

4. YOGA

If in this connection we discuss Yoga separately, it is because many people learn it without being aware that they thereby expose themselves to Hindu influences. Next to Indic mysticism, it most strongly impresses contemporary man. It offers itself to our harried and torn people initially as an aid to relaxation, to concentration, and to maintenance of the ability to work and of health. It appears harmless, a mere series of exercises, but it leads people without their noticing it into a new spiritual world and into a new form of religion. It claims to make man forget, be it only for a short time, to free him from the world of his senses, and to give him complete happiness. Yoga is a religion and is developing itself into one of the largest ersatz religions in the Christian sphere. It already recommends itself as a means toward the solution of all problems of life:

Yoga wishes more or less to mean a way which leads to a goal, a teaching which prepares us for something.

Now one of the teachings of Yoga will even help us to remain independent of all that, to cultivate the real self, the God in us, for our soul indeed carries all the characteristics of the divine. Since it is absolute and immortal, since it is subject to no conditions or limitations

[3] *Ibid.*, p. 141.

and is not bound to space, time, or causality, we must seek to come as close as possible to this soul, to this absolute, and to escape everything non-essential that surrounds us.[4]

Yoga is thus a religion and has an avowed religious goal.

In India there are five kinds of Yoga; among us only three are taught, among them primarily Hatha-Yoga, which consists of breathing exercises and gymnastics by which man is to be made able so to rule his body that it no longer affects his spirit. Thereby the spirit becomes free for concentration. As Herbert tells us, this stage is not without danger. Many people receive bodily harm from it. He therefore advises against learning it by oneself. The other stages demand such energy that people mostly refrain from them. Kriya-Yoga [Raja-Yoga] gives man the knowledge of unity with the world and with the divine. Man is thereby freed of all desires. Beside this there is Bhakti-Yoga through which man finds unity with the divine.

What is this Yoga business all about? Blanke gives the answer to this:

The exertion of spirit to achieve salvation. Through his own spiritual efforts man should rise up in order ultimately to unite mystically with the divine. Yoga is therefore self-salvation, a path from here below to above. The Christian way of salvation leads from above to here below. Only the grace which God gives us in Christ brings us into contact with God.[5]

In addition it should not remain unmentioned that many people do not become happier through the practice of Yoga, but often fall into depressions.

Since Yoga is influencing people so strongly today, the Catholic church is already seeking to make Yoga useful to itself. There are attempts to build up a Christian Yoga for meditation.[6]

[4] Jean Herbert, *Wege zum Hinduismus,* trans. Emma von Prelet (Zurich: Rascher, 1951), pp. 96, 119.
[5] Fritz Blanke, "Asiatische Religiöse Strömungen in Europa," in *Die Einheit der Kirche und die Sekten* (Zollikon: Evangelischer Verlag, 1957), p. 102.
[6] J. M. Dechanet, *Yoga für Christen: Die Schule des Schweigens* (Luzerne: Räber, 1957).

It is expressly pointed out that Yoga is shot through with the atheistic or pantheistic systems of India. Through Yoga, however, man becomes more open toward God. He is made capable of realizing the highest. Yoga releases from the world. The exercises make it possible for man to realize his own ego and God in him. He can close himself to all attractions. His ego is brought into the right relationship to Brahma. In spite of this the author comes to the conclusion that Yoga in itself is neutral. It depends upon the content given to it. In the Christian church, however, it is at best a two-edged sword.

Various groups are working today for the expansion of Yoga. The Divine Life Society, founded by the Indian Swami Sivananda, has more than five hundred branches. It espouses above all the spread of the spiritual experience of India and the unity of religion, and wishes to lead its followers to a divinely permeated service to mankind. Sivananda also founded the first Yoga university in Reshikesh, India. There students assemble from all over the world to learn Yoga. From there they again go out into the world to open teaching centers. They honor Sivananda as an incarnation of the divine. The holy one remains in continuous contact with the students through his writings. For him Yoga is the means toward moral perfection of man in union with the divine.[7] Yoga schools are found today in Zurich, St. Gallen, Lindau, and Stuttgart. In addition one finds in all the larger health resorts persons who offer to help the guests by Yoga. In Harpoldingen, in the vicinity of Säckingen, there is the "German Vedanta Center." The Zurich school publishes its own newspaper, *Yoga, Schule der Selbsterziehung [Yoga, School of Self-Education]*. The followers of Sivananda also publish a newspaper, *Yoga, Die Zeitschrift für Yoga-Synthese und Vedanta [Yoga, the Journal for Yoga Synthesis and Vedanta]*, as the official organ of the Yoga-Vedanta Academy, as well as a number of textbooks for Yoga.[8]

Along with these movements must be mentioned lesser at-

---

[7] Sri Swami Sivananda, *Dynamic Spiritual Awakening* (Calcutta), p. 8.
[8] Hutten, *op. cit.*, pp. 140 ff.

tempts to improve Germans by use of Indic thought. Generally they are not known among the larger public. Thus in Württemberg there is a "Home of Love" where one claims to acquaint people with the one God by using holy texts from all religions.

5. BAHAI

This sect is of Islamic origin. It does not attract much notice because it passes from person to person and does not demand that its members leave the church. Nevertheless it is carried along by a great awareness of mission and has many followers. Its founder, Bahaullah, designated himself as the sole bearer of revelation. It believes it can bring peace to the world. About two million persons in the world belong to it today. In Germany it has for years been pursuing the struggle to be allowed to build a second world temple in the vicinity of Frankfurt. The Bahai sect has the avowed goal of equalizing all religions. It preaches a God who can be united with reason and science, but who remains the God of Islam. It espouses peace and social justice and wishes to make one family of mankind. It believes it can do this and allow all religions to remain, but understands itself to be the perfection and goal of all religions. In personal communications and tracts it boasts not to be aggressive. It is proud of the fact that great men of many peoples are among its followers.[9]

The influence of this sect is greater than we suspect. Every urban minister runs into its influence. It is primarily its message of peace which impresses people.

6. THE LITERARY INFLUENCE

We cannot measure the influence of these sects and religions by the number of their followers, for their public influence is much larger than can be recognized from the statistics. The messengers of these religions know how to use the means of

[9] *Ibid.*, p. 139. Cf. Helmuth von Glasenapp, *Die nichtchristlichen Religionen* (Frankfurt/M: Fischer, 1957), p. 38 and Hermann Grossmann, "Die Ausbreitung und gegenwärtige Aktivität der Bahai-Religion, insbesondere in Amerika und Europa," *ZRGG*, 1958, pp. 386–398.

influencing the public. Whoever has an ear for these things must realize with a shock how very astutely the ideas of the religions are carried among the people by press and radio. That is also the case in the literary field. I refer to the work of Blanke.[10] It restricts itself, to be sure, to intellectual works. The influence is much stronger in popular literature.

There are today publishing houses which exist upon the publications of such religions and sects and do a right brisk business. We should see that today people are strongly attached to faraway things and tend to the exotic in the spiritual realm. That becomes particularly clear to us in the popular series of writings which includes monographs about the religions and has a market which surpasses that of the Christian books. Included here are many travel books and descriptions of foreign countries, best sellers in the book market.

These facts should cause us to think. They show us how little Christianity still influences the people. Is this not due to the fact that we Christians and theologians take the questions of men too lightly and therefore attempt no answer? When we do, however, we write so that men can derive nothing from it. We must find a new way to reach men if we wish to preserve them in the Christian faith.

We are come today to a point where the ground has been prepared for the foreign religions. They have it easy in our territory because our people are already familiarized with their intellectual heritage. We have played too long with these things or have permitted people to play with them. Today the time has come to ask ourselves what we propose to do.

7. THE MISSION OF HINDUISM

Until recently Hinduism was not a missionary religion. It limited its spread to the Indic peoples. Since the successful incursion of Islam into India, Hinduism has not been able to reestablish religious unity. In the middle ages there was a Hindu expansion toward Indonesia. Today a spontaneous expansion is

[10] Blanke, *op. cit.*, pp. 104–105.

taking place in Africa through the many Indian merchants. In India the presence of Islam has always forced the people to keep watch over the condition of Hinduism.

The awakening of Hinduism to missionary activity came from individuals who sought to permeate the people with their beliefs, chiefly the leaders of the Brahma Samaj and the Arya Samaj. Early among them, Debendra Nath Tagore sent out missionaries. In 1887 the Ramakrishna Mission was founded. It had its center in Belur near Calcutta, but today it has established many branches and has spread over all of India. The real missionary activity began with Vivekananda. He received the impression in Chicago that Western man was very receptive to Indic thought. Vivekananda developed an active propaganda campaign and founded three monasteries in India for the training of missionaries. Only through their activity did the desire for missionary work to influence other people awaken in Hinduism. The missionaries sought followers in Europe and America and brought them together in so-called Vedanta societies. They did not often appear publicly; nevertheless, through them the Western world came under the influence of India.

The missionary zeal of Hinduism was strengthened by the activity of Gandhi. He lived under the impression that Christianity had fallen before the ideology of force. Therefore he claimed that for the good of mankind the West must be conquered spiritually by India. He conceived his teaching of nonviolence as an article of Hindu faith, but made it a valid principle for all men. He established the proposition that this teaching could be spread only by faithful followers. Thereby Gandhi gave the Indian people a mandate.[11]

This missionary zeal received a new impetus in the disillusionment of many Europeans with Christianity and the message of the church. From all the Western world men came to India seeking to find an answer to their questions. The visit to the Ashram of Sri Aurobindo has become an example of this. To this came more than a thousand Americans, Englishmen, French-

[11] Wolff, *Indiens Beitrag . . .* , p. 67.

men, Germans, and others "who here make the overpowering
discovery that spirit is not idea and principle, but reality: creative, dynamic transformed power." Aurobindo said, "I am
here to establish the divine life and divine consciousness in those
who of themselves feel the call to come to me and to carry
on to the end." He made such an impression on these people
that already "Sri Aurobindo Circles have been formed for the
spread of such universal impulses" in England, America, France,
Greece, Holland, Italy, Israel, China, Malaya, East Africa, and
Mexico.[12]

Through the Ramakrishna Mission the attention of India was
turned upon the religious receptivity of the West. It sent a stream
of preachers to the West.

A study of their reports shows a multitude of activities: the building
of hospitals, polyclinics, and schools for women and girls; economic
development and relief. With this, emphasis is laid upon the dissemina-
tion of spiritual and cultural ideals of Hinduism. It is significant that
this occurred not only as "inner mission" activity; there is a growing
"foreign mission" activity at various places in Burma, Ceylon, Singa-
pore, Fiji, Mauritius, in the U.S.A., Argentina, England, France and
Germany.[13]

Since this missionary activity seeks to win over Christians, the
question arises how it squares with the thesis of the equality of
all religions.

Sometimes they have been justified by their advocates with the claim
that, in contrast to Christian missions, they do not attempt to make
converts, but only to make better Episcopalians, or Methodists, or the
like. But the word "better" in this connection means "hinduized," and
the purpose is clearly to bring about acceptance of a Hindu view of
life and of religion.[14]

Another mission, the Gaudiya Mission, goes back to Krishna
Chaitanya, a zealous follower of Krishna and Radha, who lived

[12] *Ibid.*, pp. 108–109.   [13] *CMS Newsletter, op. cit.*, p. 2.
[14] Charles W. Forman, "Freedom of Conversion in India," *IRM,* XLV
(1956), p. 182.

in the sixteenth century. He pronounced the name of the Indic savior Krishna so often he fell into an ecstasy and with his followers sang songs full of feeling to the praise of Krishna. He represented an enthusiastic piety. His sect survived through the centuries. Around 1900 it succeeded in winning a few followers in America. In 1934 it took up missionary attempts in Europe. It wanted to bring the theistic philosophy of India close to the Europeans.

Since 1955 there has also been an official missionary society of Hinduism.

As recently as May, 1955 a former chief justice of the supreme court of India called for the organization of Hinduism on missionary lines, employing trained evangelists; and the Vice-President of the country has expressed the hope that Hinduism will reach out into all the world to make its influence felt.[15]

Thus we are confronted by the fact that the missionary activity of Hinduism will really only now be developing.

8. BUDDHISM

Buddhism is an old missionary religion whose founder spread his teachings himself. He also instructed his monks how they were to spread the teaching. Buddhism won India and the countries of southeast Asia by a peaceful mission. Its monks spread the teaching in China and Japan and thus, in the modified form of Mahayana Buddhism, penetrated the peoples of east Asia. The period of its greatest spread was under Emperor Asoka in the third century B.C., in India. He succeeded in uniting all of India with the help of this religion. He regarded it as his prime duty to promote Buddhism everywhere through the building of temples, stupas [burial shrines], and monasteries. Asoka even sent missionaries to the Near East. Since then it has been the noblest duty of Buddhist rulers and governments to support the spread and maintenance of Buddhism. This has not always

---

[15] *Ibid.*, p. 183. Cf. Hutten, *op. cit.*, pp. 140 ff., Otto Wolff, "Die religiöse Aktivität des modernen Hinduismus," *ZRGG*, 1958, pp. 299–316, and Ernst Benz, "Hinduistische und buddhistische Missionszentren in Indien, Ceylon, Burma und Japan," *ZRGG*, 1958, pp. 333–363.

worked out for the best interests of this religion. Much stagnation can be discovered in the history of Buddhism.

When the Mohammedans invaded India in the twelfth century, the Hindus used the opportunity to drive Buddhism out of India again. They succeeded all the more easily because the Indic peoples were dissatisfied with Buddhism as an atheistic religion, and over the centuries the stronger Brahman teachings had made it inwardly hollow. So India was lost to Buddhism except for small remnants. In the other countries, however, Buddhism remained a great spiritual power which is being particularly effective again today.

Buddhism has understood how to achieve a feeling of solidarity among its people and how to make the teachings of Buddha the common property of men even though its teachings about salvation were practiced only by the monks. These always exercised a great influence because they had to go among the people for their sustenance. Recently their numbers have again increased considerably. In Burma, there are fifty thousand monks among nineteen million inhabitants; in Thailand, one hundred sixty-five thousand among nineteen million; in Ceylon, twelve to fifteen thousand among eight million; in Cambodia, four thousand among three million; and in Laos, two thousand monks among one million people.[16] Under the necessity of political development, the monastic system was reformed. Today the monasteries are the centers of education and influence. The monks learn foreign languages, study social questions, occupy themselves with other religions, and thus prepare themselves for service to their people and for spreading Buddhism. At the same time there is no stinting of meditation.

The new period, the freedom of the peoples, has brought the monks new duties and political ones. Thus Burma was rescued, to the inner gratification of the people, by the intervention of monks. In Ceylon, the monks developed such an influence that they control the results of elections. This politicalization of re-

[16] S. Kulandran, *Resurgent Religions* ("World Evangelism Today," No. 1 [London: Lutterworth Press, 1957]), p. 18.

ligion as a means of national unification does not always work
out in the best interests of Buddhism. The successes of the monks,
however, give hope to the Buddhist countries that communism
will win no influence. Through the awakening Buddhism has
experienced since World War II, its spread has begun again
along the border areas. India, especially, is to be won back
again. It became clear from the Buddha Jubilee, at which India
gave back the old shrines to the Buddhists, that Buddha belongs
even today among the Indian saints and in the Indian culture.
Even though the missionary activity of Buddhism is displeasing
to the Hindus, no one wishes to do anything against the propaganda of the Buddhists because of the common source of the
two religions. This propaganda makes a very strong impression
upon the outcastes, who even yet represent a restless herd. According to the Hindus, it is better that the outcastes become
Buddhists than that they ally themselves with Christianity. Thus
the late Dr. Ambedkar succeeded in leading six hundred thousands outcastes into Buddhism in 1957. Naturally through this
conversion they have not yet become Buddhists, but they now
stand under the influence of Buddhism. Since 1932 there has
been a Buddhist union in Indonesia. Its influence, however, is
not yet great.[17]

Buddhism also has the desire of winning back the Christians
in Buddhist countries. Everywhere it is the religion protected
by law. Going over to the Buddhists naturally brings advantages
to the Christians, for they are treated as socially inferior by the
representatives of the non-Christian religions. Thus in recent years
in Burma, there have been more Christian Karens who have gone
over to Buddhism than heathen Karens who have been won over
to Christianity. In Ceylon, Buddhism sees Christianity as its
great rival, and therefore makes a great deal of anti-Christian
propaganda. It is not as bad in East Asia where Buddhism is
only one religion among many. Yet even there much activity is
directed against the Christian church by Buddhism.

The influence of Buddhism in the West cannot be determined

[17]*Einsicht,* 1958, p. 28.

statistically. We know that since Schopenhauer the educated have always had a weakness for Buddhism because it supplies a complete philosophical system. In addition theosophy has made Buddhism's ideal of piety attractive to Western man. In Germany the first Buddhist organization was founded in 1903; in England the influence of Buddhism began in 1906. Various societies were founded and Buddhist rules for living were published for the English. Nevertheless, there are supposedly only eight hundred registered Buddhists in England. According to Manikam, Buddhism has 130 mission stations in the United States. Its activity is shown in the fact that the first Buddhist academy founded in the Western area is in New York. In France there are three hundred Buddhists; in Germany there are said to be ten thousand, which, however, fall into several feuding groups. There are congregations in Berlin, Munich, Uting, Düsseldorf, Frankfurt am Main, Cologne, and Hamburg. The Buddhist societies work through the publication of popular literature and newspapers. It is reported that each year hundreds of seekers come to the representatives of the societies and ask to be given instruction. Buddhism is passed from person to person. One can give the German Buddhists credit for carrying on the conversation with great objectivity. They exhibit a great scientific interest, research old Buddhist literature, and translate texts which are not yet known.

The Buddhist Conze regrets that up until now Buddhism has not been able to win through in the West. He attributes this to the fact that until now Buddhism has been a religion without organization. It has only the congregations of monks, but there are no such congregations in Germany. "Monks and monasteries are the indispensable foundation of a Buddhist movement, which aims at being a concrete, living reality."[18] Until now it has been difficult to build monasteries in Europe. Any German who feels himself drawn to the monastic life flees this country and goes to Ceylon or Japan.

[18] Edward Conze, *Buddhism: Its Essence and Development* (New York: Philosophical Library, 1951), p. 212.

A further development has begun here in the last few years. While up to 1956 there had been only one Buddhist missionary society, Maha Bodhi in Ceylon (founded 1891) which had as its immediate goal the reinstatement of Buddha's teachings in Buddhist lands and later sent missionaries to the West, at the Buddhist World Council a special missionary society was founded for Germany, the Lanka Dhammaduta Society, with capital funds of over two hundred thousand dollars. The missionary work in Germany was made the responsibility of Ceylon, where the Mission House was opened on August 7, 1956, by the Ceylonese prime minister. It has space for fourteen monks, and a good library which includes German literature. A German and a Swiss monk are co-operating in training missionaries. Mission methods are being studied from Christian literature. "Mission festivals" are already being held in Ceylon. The society has sent to Germany the first three monks, who immediately settled themselves in the rebuilt temple in Berlin-Frohnau. They are to move to a monastery where missionaries for Germany will be trained. A number of such monasteries are planned.[19]

Buddhism seems to be making up what it formerly lacked in the area of organization. In Germany the various Buddhist societies have banded together in the German Buddhist Society, whose goal is to further the association of the groups with one another, to watch over the attitude of the public toward Buddha's teaching, and to represent the interests of Buddhism as well as to foster communication with her motherlands.[20] This last is made easier by a further organization. In 1945 the Conference of the World Fellowship of Buddhists was founded; it has met regularly since 1950. In addition there has been a Buddhist cultural conference since 1952.

"The East in no way relates this sending of Buddhist monks into Western countries to the intention of penetrating into the spiritual and religious life of the West."[21] The Western Buddhists

[19] *Einsicht*, 1957, pp. 27, 154.　　[20] *Einsicht*, 1956, p. 158.
[21] *Einsicht*, 1957, p. 27.

are to be strengthened, however, so that they can give seekers
the possibility of finding an answer through Buddha. The monks
are to be messengers of peace and offer help in overcoming
materialism to the many in the West who are without a religion.
They are to take "the cut and well-used stones of Buddhist principles . . . [and build them] into the Temple of Western thought
as the awakening West has need of them."[22] What is that,
however, but a penetration into the spiritual life of the West?

Buddhism today makes an impression upon Western man
because it emphasizes suffering and makes an earnest effort to
deal with it. It goes beyond materialism. It insists that each
person can save himself and gives in addition a psychological
analysis. Psychology, however, has become a substitute for religion today. Buddhism is not interested in God. Man therefore
does not have to direct himself to a higher power. Man can make
amends for his mistakes by a life arranged according to the
teaching of Buddha.

9. ISLAM

Christianity has forgotten that Islam was once her archenemy.
Since the warlike confrontation has ceased, the interest of
Christianity in Islam has diminished. If any religion has a
"wild missionary faith," it is Islam. Its message of the one God
to whom all men are subject, and of the Islamic brotherhood,
which encompasses all who have submitted to this God, makes
all Moslems witnesses and missionaries of the teaching. Islam
is a missionary religion whether it sends out missionaries or not.
It has not only subjugated peoples by holy wars, but won them
by peaceful expansion. Islam has always had spontaneous
expansion, through which it has developed into the greatest
competitor to Christianity in Africa. Islam does not tear men
out of their social solidarity, but strengthens their community
through the commands of the Koran. That makes it attractive.

[22] Christmas Humphreys, *Buddhism* (Harmondsworth: Penguin Books,
1958), p. 231. Cf. Hutten, *op. cit.*, pp. 149 ff., Max Ladner, "Buddhistische
Mission in Europa," ZRGG, 1958, pp. 312–332, and Benz, *op. cit.*, pp. 333–
363.

While Christianity was continually torn apart by its quarreling peoples, thus giving the world the worst example of a religion, Islam, despite its various states and sects, remained a united religion which understood how to influence the life of its peoples. In it, too, there are believers of all races and cultures. They have as a common bond, however, the belief in Allah and the law laid down in the Koran which regulates the relationship of the believers to one another. Thus a great world brotherhood has arisen. Each Moslem is aware of belonging to a great whole. This brotherhood has its center in Mecca, whence stimuli reach out to the faithful in the most distant lands. At the university El Azhar, men are educated for all Moslem countries. It is the brain of Islam. Thus despite the diversity of its peoples, Islam binds its believers together.

It has also gone through long periods of decline. Today it is again awake. It has succeeded in again setting up the "house of Islam" through liberation from colonial rule. Today the *corpus islamicum* is still in question in only a few places. This fact gives the Moslems a new impetus. The external success is regarded as proof of the fact that Allah desires to use his people for great tasks. Through political success the Islamic world not only has become aware of itself, but also is on the way to winning back the old fanaticism. The conviction has once again established itself that Allah helps those who fight for his honor.

The countries of Egypt, Turkey, Pakistan, and Indonesia want to be democratic. The Moslems have not succeeded in setting up the government so as to make Islam the one legal religion. In the thinking of the peoples, however, this conviction is present. Non-Moslem missionary activity is as little permitted even in Malaya as it is in the central Arabic regions. So far, Christians are treated as second-class citizens; therefore every year some Christians go over to Islam. In many countries, as in the Sudan and the Celebes, there are forced conversions to Islam. It is true: Islam knows no mercy!

The missionary activity of the Moslems occurs primarily through continual and spontaneous expansion. In Indonesia, since

1912, the Mohammedaniyya, a puritanic missionary sect modeled after the Wahabis, has attempted to imitate Christian missionary activity. It works primarily in the social, educational, health, and literary fields. Another organized missionary activity in East Africa is carried on by the Ismailis of India. It was undertaken by the Aga Khan and is carried on today by his followers. It, too, emphasizes school work. Contrast to the white race is emphasized and the Negro is stimulated to nationalism. In Africa, the Ahmadiyya is also at work. It does not limit itself, as the other orders do, to the winning of heathen, but has declared the whole world its mission field.

All organized missionary movements of Islam proceed from India and without doubt are related to the revitalization of Hinduism. The Ahmadiyya was founded in 1890 by Mirza Ghulam Ahmad (1835-1908). He held himself to be the savior of the world. He lived in the conviction that he had the command of Allah to spread his kingdom in peaceful fashion. He modernized and de-politicized his orders and gave his followers high ethical rules, completely binding them to the Koran, which he explained in a modern way. At the same time he held himself to be the caliph and thus the supreme head and spiritual leader of Islam. Since he also claimed to be the Mahdi, the reform of Islam had to be as near to his heart as its spread. In this he ran into the obstinate opposition of the orthodox, who nevertheless did not dare exclude him. It is significant that despite the many quarrels over doctrine within Islam, no excommunication occurred.

The sects flirted a great deal with England in order to win greater influence in India, and procured for themselves in addition a great mission center in the Wocking Mosque in London, to which a number of leading Englishmen belong.

Today the Ahmadiyya has mission posts in all the larger cities of the world from which it also works through literature. The posts also receive foreign Moslems. In heathen regions, as for example in West Africa, it seeks to win people through social activity and school work. It understands how to use the situation and proceeds with greatest arrogance. As has already been said, it takes from each of its members the vow to spread Islam.

Along with the Ahmadiyya, Sufism has sought to influence Europe. It was called into being by the Indian Inayot Khan. He wished to unite all religions because the same God is worshiped in all religions. His worship services were comprised of readings from all religions. He wanted a universal "church," which would embrace all confessions and religions and in which no one would need to give up his confession of faith.[23] Sufism is related to Persian mysticism. It represents no further danger for Christianity.

For America, the Ahmadiyya has its centers in Chicago and Buenos Aires; for Europe, in London, Hamburg, Zurich, Paris, and Helsinki. It makes a strong impression upon the Negroes in America because it demands equal justice. In the European countries the Ahmadiyya chiefly gathers the existing Moslems, though some Europeans do go over to Islam. In Berlin, in the years from 1929 to 1939, there is said to have been an average of one conversion each month. The largest Moslem group is in France, where they are said to number three hundred fifty thousand. The figures for Germany are set at thirty-three hundred, among whom eight hundred are said to be Germans. One of the secretaries of the Islamic World Youth Organization is a German.[24] Without question, the influence of Islam is growing because through foreign workers and students the building of new congregations is constantly taking place. The Ahmadiyya has congregations in Germany in Hamburg, Berlin, Munich, Nürnberg and Neu-Ulm, and in the Ruhr. Through the modern translation of the Koran, with its strong attack on Christian revelation, the sect is acquiring influence today among college students.

To close this chapter, we should like to clarify from our confession of faith where the differences between Christianity and

[23] Blanke, *op. cit.*, p. 100. Cf. Abu Bakr Siraj al-Din, *The Book of Certainty* (London: Rider, 1952).
[24] J. Goettin, "Vom neuen Leben in der islamischen Welt Indonesiens," *EMM*, 1957, p. 146.

Islam lie. The portions set aside in parentheses are the utterances which Islam totally denies:

"I believe in God, (the Father) almighty, maker of heaven and earth:

And in Jesus Christ, (his only Son, our Lord), who was conceived by the Holy Spirit, born of the virgin Mary, (suffered under Pontius Pilate, was crucified), dead (?), (and buried: he descended into hell, the third day he rose from the dead), he ascended into heaven, (and is seated on the right hand of God, the Father almighty), whence he shall come (to judge the living and the dead).

I believe in the Holy Ghost, (the holy Christian church, the communion of saints), the forgiveness of sins, the resurrection of the body, and the life everlasting."[25]

---

[25] Alfred Guillaume, *Islam* (Harmondsworth: Penguin Books, 1956), p. 194. Cf. Hutten, *op. cit.*, pp. 122 ff.

6

Our Reply

1. THE FALSE CLAIM

Our answer should not serve as self-justification. That would be a sign of our blindness, complacency, and lack of contrition. On the other hand, for the sake of truth, we must test whether the statements of other religions and their claim that they train and mold their people better than Christianity are correct. Are they really superior to Christianity in this way, as they claim?

The task will be difficult for us because both Hinduism and Buddhism are religions which are not historically oriented, which are not interested in the past of their peoples, but which always think in terms of personal karma. They are classic examples of the fact that where God is not understood as the creator and upholder of mankind, there is no sense of history. Only the personal God provides a basis for history, makes it advance with mankind, and brings it to its goal. Where the world is regarded as a prison which man must escape, on the other hand, everything that happens in the world must be regarded as illusion. Therefore man cannot have any historical interest. We therefore cannot expect that in the lands of these religions everything would be accurately established chronologically. These people first acquired an interest in history through the colonial powers and through Christianity, which, phenomenologically evaluated, is by its very nature a historical religion.

It was Christianity which first brought to these peoples the conditions for historical judgments. It gave them the standard for correctly evaluating events and for giving up religious prejudices. The peoples learned very quickly; today they turn these standards against Christianity—without giving the impression that they have subjected themselves to the same principles. Naturally high moral principles are also present in the other religions, but they are not absolute. They have always been limited by the teaching of karma and disturbed by the interwoven tribal relationships of the people, which can be used to excuse a great deal. Was the moral superiority of the East over the West always assumed? Up until the religions had been perfected by Christianity, certainly not.

If we first take up the reproach of our use of force and our desire for power, then we must allow ourselves to be told—and we should not erase this mirror image—that the white race through its continual warlike disputations and its economic expansion has become a scourge to mankind. This general verdict seems unfair in two ways. The good the colonial powers have done for the peoples is taken into consideration only to a small extent. They were the powers which established order and through their objective justice, through building up commerce, through introducing better methods of work, and through their school system brought about the conditions that enabled the peoples in question to become free. If the white man is losing his power in the East today, no one should blame the young nations for it, but if those nations confiscate his property, often in the hands of one family for hundreds of years, and abandon him to mobs, these sins contradict the principles of the "morally better" religions.

Furthermore: The Asiatic peoples, too, fought their wars. Here, too, there is no excusing that the Christians have torn one another apart and that the whole world has been pulled into their quarrels. If, however, these religions think in cycles, they should consider that Asia again and again was the strongest threat to Europe, and that at a time when its people had already become acquainted with Buddhism.

Islam, too, was for centuries the nightmare of Europe. In the history of the lands where these religions began, things did not always go peaceably. Not only have the Mohammedan alignments struggled with one another for supremacy, but also despite the teaching of non-violence there were always wars in India between the various states.

Nor has Hinduism shaken off the will to power. When Conze[1] says that in the Buddhist territory there have been only two major wars, over which Buddhists are still ashamed today, he does not mention that within the various countries war for power has always been carried on. It would seem that according to the teaching of non-violence, only wars with other powers are condemned. History has proved, since 1945, that even Hindus and Buddhists can fight. When it was a matter of India's advantage, even Gandhi could justify fighting, and Nehru could attack in Kashmir. We do not say that to justify ourselves, but only to establish that despite his highly exalted belief, the Hindu or the Buddhist remains subject to evil—speaking from a Christian standpoint, subject to sin—and his own ego is often stronger in him than his sympathy with all forms of life. At any rate it is a very questionable sign when Ceylon shows the highest crime rate in the world.

Another one-sided reproach states: The Christian mission has always grown with the expansion of Western power and has been a means of Western expansion. For this, too, there are, of course, specific examples and we are aware that it should not have been so. The men who raise these objections count on man's having a very short memory. Naturally missions and politics were sometimes closely related. Missions could not have established themselves, in many countries, if the way had not already been cleared. But no case can be cited where the land was forced

[1] Edward Conze, *et al.* (trans. and ed.), *Buddhist Texts Through the Ages* (New York: Philosophical Library, 1957), p. 15.

open for the sake of missions! Furthermore there are countless examples where the missionary initiative had succeeded long before the colonial power appeared. Many examples could be cited where a mission supported the natives against a colonial power. The relationship between politics and missions is not so easy to describe as many would have it.

If we survey the world religions, we find no separation of the religions from government. In their countries, religious compulsion and political force have often enough been united. The spread of Hinduism and Buddhism did not occur without their governments. The governments built the shrines and monuments. The Buddhist kings were always patrons of the faith. The famous Asoka did everything to spread Buddhism, and so did Kanishka. If Buddhism penetrated China and Japan peaceably, the fact should not be overlooked that often enough the monks wooed the favor of the rulers in order to reach their goal. Today, too, the view is again prevalent in Buddhist lands that religion and nation must coincide.

Let us briefly throw light on the social area. The Buddhist proclaims sympathy with all living things. The Hindu also protects animals. But who in their countries has protected the people from social exploitation? No one. Even today the tenants are so treated by the landowners that they cannot achieve their freedom. Was it not true in India that the powerful could do anything they wished, while those placed lower socially must suffer everything? Even today, if a tenant frees himself from his landowner he may have to leave the area, because it can be arranged that he finds no further work. The colonial power first brought social principles to India. The contrasts were perpetuated by the caste system, which is also a religious arrangement. How does all this fit in with spiritualization and setting man free from his self? Are these facts not proof that Hinduism itself has no deep effect?

It is similar in Islam, which extols the Koran as the social law for mankind. The Ahmadiyya even proclaims that it fights slavery. Nonetheless, the oriental lands are still alive with slavery. To be sure, each Mohammedan finds equality of rights and security in the family group, but what happens to the alien? What about the exploitation of the pilgrims in Mecca? We have the impression that abuses occur in these religions as in Christianity. Men know exactly what they should do; whether it is done, however, depends upon whether man takes his religion seriously. The other religions have only the advantage that their peoples have not yet gone through the experience of individualism. Their people are carried by tradition. But will it always remain so?

Today the other religions claim to have *the* answer to the many questions of men. It is interesting that their message always begins at the point where the church has not spoken: with social justice and peace. We can understand the claim of Islam on the basis of the origin of its revelation. We must dismiss it in the case of the other religions, for in them not God, but man's desire for salvation is the decisive factor. They proceed from the viewpoint that this desire for salvation must be present everywhere and that as a result the question of human existence must be a burning issue among all men. They believe also that the Indic solutions have validity for all men. If this were true, we should have to ask why Hindus and Buddhists did not spread their religion long ago? Why in the territories of these religions is there, alongside the pious and learned, a mass of people who can make nothing of the philosophical solutions. What is recommended to us by both religions is basically suitable only for individuals. Buddha even said this himself, and the German Buddhists admit it. "To be sure the teaching of Buddha is not suited for the great masses. Buddha knew from the outset that most people would not understand."[2] Can such religions make a claim to all mankind? What good is it if a few understand the teaching, but the people are left alone in their distress? How completely different at this point is the teaching of Jesus, which offers the deepest satisfaction to the simple man just as much as to the learned man, a teaching which is concerned with proclaiming salvation and thus the glad tidings to all men.

[2] Kurt Schmidt, "Buddha und die Gegenwart," *Einsicht*, 1956, p. 105.

The Gospel is unique not only because of its revelation, but also because of its content and because of the goal of the revelation. It does not offer speculation about the existence of man, but offers the redemptive acts of God as they were executed by his Son Jesus Christ. It is not myth, but history. The content is thus a historical person, the God-man Jesus Christ himself, and the goal is not to show a few men the philosophical possibility of salvation, but to rescue all men through the historical deed of Jesus Christ. The difference from the foreign religions is here so great that one could, for instance, proclaim the teachings of Hinduism or Buddhism without mentioning the teacher. One cannot, however, proclaim the Gospel without Jesus Christ, for he is himself the content of the message.

This fact alone must make us very cautious about speaking of the dependency of the Gospel upon India. No one will deny there are common elements. Also no one will deny that in its founding years, Christianity came into contact with Indic ideas. Still, no one will succeed in proving that the content of the Gospel was taken over from India. The differences come forth most strongly precisely where the common elements seem apparent. The things seemingly held in common are only a proof that the witnesses of the Gospel have already come to grips with Indic thought.

This fact appears in the entire biblical revelation. The Bible from the first page to the last is a confrontation of God's will for salvation with man's self-seeking struggle toward salvation, and is therefore in conflict with the temptations which the surrounding religious world presents to the people of God. The foreign religions always want to rescue autonomous man, but God is always concerned to save sinful man. The message of the religions is in complete opposition to the Gospel. This becomes especially clear today under the attack of these religions. Therefore there is no way of working together in the battle against secularism, as could still be suggested in 1928 in Jerusalem. The church must recall the uniqueness of its message and set itself in opposition to those religions.

2. THE OTHER CONCEPT OF GOD

As we have repeatedly demonstrated with regard to the other religions, the first concern is not with God, even when they speak of him, but the concern is with man's understanding of existence. They constantly wrestle with the question whether there is a real existence. This is seen as an absolute which is, however, not given, but is always recognized only insofar as the intellectual ability of man can establish it, or insofar as it can be experienced through mystic union. In identity with the divine man recognizes his own being and the world receives its characteristic existence. Therefore it is highest wisdom and knowledge when man after a wearisome journey comes to the conclusion: "I am that!" Or when he can say: "God is nature, the world, the universe. This divinity is indeed transcendent as the absolute power, but in its form of being and working it is completely immanent. It is not a person, but a power. Every visible thing is surrounded by it."

This concept of God is congruent with the understanding of revelation. As the absolute is eternal, without beginning or end, so also is the world as an emanation of the divine, so is man with his uncreated soul, so are the Vedas and other holy writings. Everything has proceeded from the divine and everything returns to the divine. It is a great cycle in which there can basically be neither space nor time, and thus also there can be no historical intervention by God.

It is completely different in Christian revelation. In it God is given *a priori*. He creates the world and reveals himself by dealing with this world and speaking to men. God and the world are not one, but stand over against one another. Here God does not express himself in himself alone as is the case according to the Indic conception, but reveals himself to another; he reveals himself in such a way that always something hidden and unascertainable is revealed. Thus man cannot recognize God by reflecting upon himself, but must be told who God is and what man is. There can only be revelation, in this sense of the word, when God reveals himself to his opposite.

This does not mean that there is no revelation in the non-

Christian religions. Anyone who has read Karl Barth's classic monograph about revelation[3] knows that there are possibilities of extra-Christian revelation. We should be very cautious, however, of speaking of revelation in this doubtful way, for what is present in the other religions by way of "revelation" can only become clear to him who lets his judgment be determined by Christian revelation:

If the revelation in Christ is well understood, the eye is opened for the depravity and perversion of human religious life which occur in the non-Christian religions and in empirical Christianity, and no weak or meek judgment will be pronounced. The eye is also opened for the deep aspirations and longings and magnificent embodiment of these longings and aspirations. Nevertheless, in the light of this revelation in Christ and in the light of what *God* has wrought through it, all things necessarily undergo a drastic re-evaluation and recreation.[4]

According to Karl Barth, Christian revelation is an event which is necessary to man's life, affirms him, is necessary for his salvation, is eternal and valid for the men of all times, reveals to man what is hidden from him and is necessary to his salvation, is fulfilled in time, and can be imitated by no man. This revelation is outside the sphere of human competence. Man can only hear it and obey it.

In Christian revelation, God stands at the beginning, in the middle, and at the end. It is always the same God who steps into history through his revelation, creates men, saves them, and makes them whole. He is not to be realized through speculations, but is recognizable only insofar as he approaches man as Creator and Lord, as Savior and God of Mercy. He is the Lord of the world and of men. Over against him everything is only creation, the creature, which lives by his benevolence. World and man have their source in God, but they are not one with him, but are

---

[3] Karl Barth, *Das christliche Verständnis der Offenbarung* ("Theologische Existenz heute," Nr. 12 [Munich: Chr. Kaiser]. Cf. *Revelation,* ed. John Baillie and Hugh Martin (New York: The Macmillan Company, 1937), pp. 41–81.

[4] Hendrik Kraemer, *The Christian Message in a Non-Christian World* (New York: Harper & Bros., 1938), pp. 128–129.

the object of his love and care. God has so revealed himself to
them that with his creature, with man, he speaks as with a Thou.
He has so created man that he can listen to Him and can obey
Him. Here man in his search for God cannot remain imprisoned
in his own ideals. God himself tells him who he is. In the last
analysis, the Indic religions always concern themselves only with
man and therefore carry on a monolog. In the Gospel, man is
addressed by God through the Word of God; he must reply to it;
thus there arises the relationship of a dialog.

God begins the history of the world in the creation and carries
it forward in his preservation. He takes man completely into this
history. He does not work as a dynamic power in everything, but
has placed within his creatures the vital and creative possibility
to remain in opposition to him. In this he demands two things
from man: (1) Man shall be obedient to Him. Through obedience man remains in the right relationship to God, in the proper
association which forms the basis for his existence. Man remains
true man only so long as he recognizes God as his Lord and
Creator and does not through disobedience step outside of this
position over against God. (2) The obedience of man always
takes place in and toward the world created by God. Man shall
cultivate the earth and have dominion over it. Thus he is called
to work and challenged to efforts of his spirit. He receives a
cultural imperative and thus stands in history under a divine
mandate:

Man is thus, by his ability to engender culture, a creator in a
secondary sense. God gives him his blessing in this mission. This mandate and blessing imply a personal relationship. Man is God's servant,
partner and co-worker, and God is his Lord and Employer![5]

The Indic man can recognize no other task in the world than to
lead the world to its real being by identification with the divine.
He must find unity with the divine in order to become its instrument. The Christian on the other hand is man in the complete

[5] Kraemer, *Religion and the Christian Faith* (Philadelphia: Westminster
Press, 1956), p. 247.

sense; he places himself under the authority of his Lord, he accepts a mandate, and in carrying it out he has a part in God's shaping of history.

Here the ethic is not a piece of personal soul cultivation as in Hinduism, nor is it a means of salvation as in Buddhism; here ethical activity confirms the God-relationship in the midst of the world. Thus man carries co-responsibility for the world. This is all the more possible since the Word of God, because of the sins of man, is always a critic of culture. He cannot create unrestrainedly, but must always put himself at the disposal of God's plans. The goal is thus not to make the world divine as in India, but according to God's mandate to make the world God's world. God remains God and the world remains the world. Despite their modification, the Indic religions remain stuck here in the basic monistic conception; they have sunk back again below what they borrowed from the Gospel.

We know that man has fallen away from the mandate of God because he has not been satisfied to be a creaturely likeness of God, but has striven toward equality with God. Man wants to be like God; that is his sin! Since the non-Christian religions make equality with God a part of their essential content, they are religions of this fall into sin. Radhakrishnan senses this himself. Therefore he fights with passion against the Christian understanding of God. If man is a part of the divine he cannot sin. Thus the foreign religions of necessity end in trying themselves to reconstitute the disturbed relationship with God, in order to make the return to God possible. They live in the knowledge of God, but are stuck fast in the human search for God:

It was the deepest insight of the Reformation that the most real and innermost character of sin is that man wants to form his own religion and in doing this he thinks to please God and to create something holy which gives him a right to community with God. For while he wants to make his religion valid before God, it is basically he who has turned away from God and has fallen as a sacrifice to idols.[6]

[6] Vilmos Vajta, "Die verborgene Heiligkeit der Kirche," in *Gedenkschrift für D. Werner Elert* (Berlin: Lutherisches Verlagshaus, 1955), p. 297.

For this religious natural man the worst is, to be sure, that God has so revealed himself that he recognizes neither another God beside himself nor this striving of men. He is the one God. Therefore he does not give man the freedom to pick a rose according to his taste from the garden of revelation. Here it is not a matter of the right and the judgment of man, but only of the judgment of God upon man, because the foolishness of God is still always far wiser than all the intelligence of men:

The religions which stand outside the biblical revelation contain truth in the form of perversion. Just as a lie lives upon truth and only arises from truth, the extra-biblical religions live from the truth of that beam of light of divine glory which has struck them.[7]

The other religions today lay great emphasis upon the fact that they demand no faith from man, but that man can verify all their statements. To believe that there is a God would contradict reason. James says: The devils also believe it and tremble. God's existence depends neither upon its being subject to proof by reason nor upon recognition by men. He is simply there. No one will succeed in proving that he does not exist. That should tell us only how cheap such an objection is. Whoever believes in God never has the feeling that he is doing something contrary to reason. Even in the other religions, one must believe; the difference from the Christian faith is only that here man is placed under obedience to God through faith, while in Hinduism and Buddhism man only believes insofar as his so-called freedom is not disturbed.

Biblical revelation denies this freedom. The pronouncements of God concerning man are: That he is a sinner and therefore cannot save himself and cannot bring himself into the right relationship to God. He must be saved by God. God, the Creator, remains true to his creation. Even fallen man is still his creature. Even the adherents of the other religions are still his creatures. God's concern, then, is to tear men away from the world of sin. His whole revelation is conditioned by God's saving activity on behalf of men. God's universal will to salvation is primarily based upon

[7] Peter Brunner, "Gotteserkenntnis," in *Gedenkschrift für D. Werner Elert* (Berlin: Lutherisches Verlagshaus, 1955), p. 268.

his faithfulness to his creation. If God claims all men and makes his salvation valid for all, he has not usurped this role, but he acts as the Lord of mankind.

3. THE NEW IMAGE OF MAN

The religions' different concept of God must also of necessity have a different concept of man, either as a condition or as a consequence. How closely the two hang together can be recognized in the fact that both Hinduism and Buddhism seek to rescue man by blaming God for the sins of the white race. Because the concept of a personal God necessitates conceiving of the personality of man as an opposite, the ego in man as he is conceived by Christians can become magnified until it takes the place of God. On the other hand, the Asiatic man understands himself as one with the divine, and thus is not at all able to turn himself against the divine. Through Asiatic religion, man is freed from his ego.

For both religions, the personality-ego is a delusion because the concept of existence is given in participation in the absolute. As a result of this, Hinduism establishes as ultimate knowledge: "I am that!" namely the absolute. Buddhism leads to the knowledge: "I am not that!" namely, not the empiric self. In either case, man is something quite different from what he appears; only the spirit of man, which enables man to analyze himself, has reality. Here man feels his condition of existence as a great burden from which he would like to free himself. He consciously will have nothing to do with the creatureliness of man. He does not care to be God's creature which has fallen into sin and is ruined. Courage is lacking to admit this, to give oneself into this dependency.

Of what then does the freedom consist of which Hindus and Buddhists are so proud? Does it exist only in independence from God? The ego which is chained to the world is in no case free. It must be made free. Whence comes the wish for freedom, which is after all a proof that even in these religions man does not feel himself free? Man is basically good. Does it not become evident in this optimism that neither religion takes seriously the evil of whose existence it is aware? This evil cannot simply be pushed out of the world by my ridding myself of desires. Since both religions understand God as immanent, but understand evil as apparently lying outside of man, they cannot understand the Christian message, which teaches the opposite. The biblical revelation, which does not concern itself with philosophical questions, but has its eye upon concrete man, knows therefore that man is a sinner and that behind his sin are still other powers to which man has subjected himself through his fall from God. Man in his sin is held so fast by these powers that he becomes the instrument of demons. Only if he lets himself be freed in Jesus Christ is he freed from serving these powers. Freeing oneself is therefore on the basis of the Scriptures impossible in a double sense: Man himself cannot restore the disrupted relationship to God, and he cannot free himself from evil by his own strength.

Biblical revelation does not thereby tell man what he would like to hear, but it is nevertheless more merciful than any non-Christian religion because it speaks the truth. Moreover the Christian teaching cannot be developed "from the depths of things, from the nature of man," although it is confirmed by the experience of believing man. The Christian revelation always comes from God. It is given through his transactions with the concrete man among the people of Israel and in the incarnation of Jesus Christ, in which God juxtaposes fallen man and the man who, without sin, was thus the real man. Only through Jesus Christ do we know what fallen man is and how the man of God is created. This man is, however, not an idea, but a historical personality. He is God's strongest confrontation directed against any spiritualizing of his creation and salvation.[8]

4. REBIRTH AND RETRIBUTION

The cry for freedom in these religions comes without question from the fact that man does not want to subordinate himself to God. "Buddhism knows no higher power which leads and directs. Here man is the focal point."[9] There is then no deeper meaning

[8] H. Meyer, "Das Evangelium in der Begegnung mit dem Mythos in Indien," EMZ, 1953, pp. 65 ff.

of history, no purposeful end to what happens. Man is responsible
for everything. Christian eschatology teaches otherwise; it is
therefore a great irritation to Hindus and Buddhists. Generally it
is held against Christianity that no ethical stimulus comes from
it. On the basis of Christian teaching, one can only say that at
precisely this point, natural man would like to flee from the final
responsibility and the decisive call to obedience. It is precisely
the eschatology which gives the final and decisive emphasis to
the Lordship of God in history. It is the end of every human glory
and self salvation, even of the "existential realization of that state
of affairs where the deepest, eternal kernel of existence of man
becomes aware of its own eternity (in the sense of the highest
and final single reality, timeless and not subject to change)."[10]
Whoever takes the final judgment in earnest receives more ethical
stimulus than man is ever in a position to give himself otherwise.

Is this Christian eschatology more contrary to reason than that
which Hinduism and Buddhism teach? The will, the decision, the
turning toward or away is decisive and what then happens is only
a process, "is a causal chain of events and as such gives results and
is inexorable."[11] That means, however, that the rolling ball set in
motion in eternity and held in motion by the law of karma, again
and again receives impetus from the deeds of men and rolls further
until the cycle of time comes to an end and the world must go
up in flames. That is the one explanation of history which Buddhism can offer, if indeed it even attempts one. No one can inter-
fere with the course of things, not even the gods themselves.
"Wisdom speaks of that lawfulness of existence which controls
reality, controls men, gods and demons, and makes up that
sequence of action by which alone the life and effort of all beings
becomes possible."[12] One must ask himself what meaning indeed
life and effort have in such a teaching? Must not the simple man
sink here completely into fatalism?

[9] Max Ladner, "Buddhistische Moral," *Einsicht,* 1956, p. 141.
[10] Winfried Petri, "Zur Geschichte und Gegenwartsbedeutung des Buddhismus," *Einsicht,* 1957, p. 174.   [11] Ladner, *loc. cit.*
[12] Hellmuth Hecker, "Der Buddhismus und das Abendland," *Einsicht,*
1957, p. 65.

Since Buddhism denies divine guidance and also does not take earnestly the reality of evil in its influence upon events, it must charge the effect of good and evil to the dynamic power of karma. That is the reason Buddhism explains suffering as a result of being born, of the ego, and of the desire for life. The teaching of karma is nothing but a primitive explanation of existence seen from the position of man over against his environment.

Man is then, as far as his fate is concerned, completely on his own. "In place of the directing God comes the law of karma, the law of cause and effect, a law of nature which no one can escape."[13] Thus the empirical existence of man is nothing but a chain of rebirths in the process of becoming and decaying, from which there is no escape. Can one even call this teaching a natural law? Every natural law is subject to proof. Here, however, no one can establish the cause for his condition, for his fateful involvement. This statement of belief can only be set up because one wishes to hold to the other belief concerning the eternity of the soul, and because death as judgment is not taken seriously. Where death is understood as a final end of life, there can be no rebirth. There is only resurrection. Because the Bible takes sin—and thus the transitoriness of man—in complete earnest, and because it knows about the creative majesty of God, it can give only resurrection as the goal of salvation. Here the Asiatic speaks of the cruel Christian God who can in the last judgment condemn to hell, and who punishes into the third and fourth generation. Is the doctrine of karma not much more cruel? In this doctrine the punishment repeats itself from birth to birth. Is it really a consolation that I receive payment for my deeds *hic et nunc?* Is there not the desire behind it not to have to present myself to the judging God?

There is a much greater consolation in the Christian doctrine of creation. Each person is a thought of God and as such unique. He does not have to bear the burden of the past; it is taken from him by forgiveness. Man does not have to make his way through the world alone carrying this burden through many lives. He is

[13] Ladner, *loc. cit.*

carried by the love of God to whom he is responsible, and to whom he may entrust his life for time and eternity. He is not one with nature. To be sure, he shares in its sighing, but he is so removed by God's love that through his salvation in Jesus Christ even nature may find peace. He is placed in the communion of those who live, as he, under the curse of sin, who also have as he in faith received salvation through the death of Christ and hope of eternal life.

Now, to be sure, Hinduism and Buddhism teach that man can by a correct approach bring the cycle of rebirth to a standstill through the realization of his knowledge. He can then stop the sequence of cause and effect. Is that not a great delusion? For instance, would the earth stop if I had realized by what it was set to spinning? I fear that despite philosophical knowledge, despite meditative depth and despite ethical seriousness, one needs in both religions a faith which cannot be attained.

5. DEIFICATION

The modification of the religions has led to no new understanding of God and man. At most the ethical struggle on the path of salvation has changed; in their insights the religions remain bound in emotion, for nothing else is possible in mysticism. The following utterance by a Buddhist says this most clearly: "Where religion begins, philosophy ends, and where we still quarrel over concepts, religion is far from having begun."[14] Until now only Christianity, with its revelation, has submitted itself to science. What would happen in the other religions if their texts were handled in the fashion that Christian theology handles biblical texts?

Even Buddhism does not get around the divine. That becomes clear in the call to the path of Buddha. For the educated, Buddha's life is solely an example, which is felt to be the unique exemplary solution of the question of existence. By the common people, however, it is understood as a substitutionary path. That is already true in southern Buddhism, but comes out especially in

[14] Erich Schmidt, "Die Welt ohne Vorstellung," *Einsicht*, 1956, p. 2.

northern Buddhism which conceives itself to be a religion of salvation and grace:

> I believe in him as the highest being; because of the sinfulness of men and because of their suffering, Amida Buddha was incarnate and came upon earth to save men; and only in his suffering love is hope to be found for me and for the world. He became human to become its savior; and no one but he alone can help. He watches constantly over all who trust in him and helps them.[15]

If one were to set Christ in place of Amida Buddha, these statements would be Christian in their formulation. Here Buddhism has turned itself into its opposite. Even in southern Buddhism one is not far from the recognition of a divine principle. The people have always prayed to Buddha. This deification becomes quite clear in the strong messianism which has seized the Buddhist world today. The religion without God hopes for the man in whom the absolute is embodied and who can turn away the sorrow of mankind. This messianism is present also, by the way, in both of the other religions, except that there men declare themselves in a positively repelling fashion to be messiahs, as for example Sivananda.[16]

In Hinduism, man is conceived to be the vessel and instrument of the divine. He carries the responsibility for his deeds only insofar as he does not place himself at the disposal of the divine. It is therefore not surprising that we scarcely find conscience mentioned in the texts of the two religions. Conscience always proves that man knows himself to be responsible to a higher power. There is conscience only where man is related to God responsibly. Christianity is an avowed religion of conscience because man knows God's law. Conscience is, however, also proof that man recognizes himself as a free personality who makes his own decisions and therefore that he knows about the responsibility which he has to bear.

---

[15] Hellmut von Schweinitz, *Buddhismus und Christentum* (*"Glauben und Wissen,"* *Nr.* 14 [Munich: Ernst Reinhardt, 1955]), p. 64.
[16] Dewan Bahadur K. S. Ramaswami Sastri, *Sivananda: The Modern World-Prophet* (Rishikesh: Yoga-Vedanta Forest University, 1953).

The Indian thinks to reach deification through Yoga and mysticism. It is significant that thinking Indians are themselves not satisfied with this system. Ramakrishna questioned the Yoga system and the theory of the unity of the all in one [monism]. Aurobindo rejected mysticism. What can be said critically against the Indic system has been best expressed by Brunton:

I found in India that the truth about the Yoga system was that, in its twentieth century practice, it was acually no system at all, for it had become as mixed as an Irish stew. It was hard to recognize what was mythical and what was mystical. Yoga had been thought largely useless to the modern world because it was held tight by fantastic faquirs in the crippling and unfortunate embrace of superstition.

This applied especially to the claim that Yoga is the way.

Thus the illuminations gained by Yoga were always temporary ones. They needed to be renewed daily at the cost of temporary renunciation of practical duties and worldly activities.

Trance is a way of escape—the body is made quiet, the physical mind is in a state of torpor, the inner consciousness is left free to go on with its experience. [Here Brunton is quoting Aurobindo.]

The price of Yoga was world-renunciation.[17]

Brunton makes similar judgments concerning mysticism:

After much arduous effort and many arduous years you reach the top of the ridge. Alas! at the fateful moment of success you discover that the real summit lies still higher and that you will have to struggle upwards again for more arduous years before it greets your gaze.

I had begun to perceive that truth lay as far beyond mysticism as the latter lay beyond religion.

The subtle exquisiteness of this state can only be appreciated by those who have actualized it in their own being. Nevertheless the vital sap which feeds the tree of mysticism is drawn up from its roots in feeling alone.

It is clear therefore that as a sole source of *certain* knowledge, mystic or yogic experience cannot be relied on.[18]

[17] Paul Brunton, *The Hidden Teaching Beyond Yoga* (New York: E. P. Dutton, 1941), pp. 32–35.   [18] *Ibid.,* pp. 58, 60, 75, 192.

It is heartening that such judgments are uttered by an earnest, striving Yogi. Kraemer judges similarly when he says that in the last analysis Indic philosophy hides its weaknesses and is unreal and false because while, to be sure, it speaks of the highest, it misuses everything, even the Divinity, for its own purposes, namely for the saving of autonomous men.[19] Basically it cannot be otherwise, for mysticism is the strongest proof that God and man are indeed not one. What in Christian revelation is brought forth as the order of creation, the relationship of the creature and creator, the community of persons, is regarded in India as the sin of ignorance to which one would like to put an end through mysticism. One wishes to be as God and thus in mysticism one always repeats again what is described as the fall into sin by the Bible.

6. SALVATION

We have now to hold up the biblical concept against this other picture of man, this fatalistic self-concept of man and his realization of the *eritus sicut deus*. In the biblical revelation, God is never the conceptual object of man; it is man who is the goal of God's love. While the claim of the Indic religions can be described as a seeking for God through which man wishes to find himself, in the Bible is revealed to us the God who seeks man, who wants to make man again what he once was: a creature of God. The salvation which God offers to man is based completely upon his position as Creator. Because he has created man, he reveals himself. Because these men have fallen away from him, he saves them. The universal salvation of God is based completely upon the creation. Because men are still his creatures today, he redeems them. With this his salvation, God at the same time rejects all attempts of man to save himself. It is then not a question of the religions' being able to offer a salvation. Only the fact that all men belong to God and he is their Lord is decisive. His love to men goes so far that he will save them himself. As the heart of

[19] Kraemer, *op. cit.*, p. 110.

his revelation, God carries out this redemption in historical deeds. Holy Scripture is not based upon the speculations of men, nor upon their ability to save themselves, but only upon the saving will of God, upon his deeds in Jesus Christ.

God's saving love shows itself first in that he does not annihilate man who has fallen into sin. He acknowledges his creatures further; he upholds them; he wishes to draw them to himself through love. That is true for all men. Even the non-Christians live by his love. Even men who have fallen prey to demons, together with the power which they honor, must live through the patience of God.

God made his salvation complete when he allowed his son to become man. He is called the image of the invisible God in Scripture. That is to say, men have to see in Jesus all that they can know of God. When Jesus became man he made clear at the same time what man is and for what God made him. Through the atoning death of Jesus, men were given their real life. This salvation reaches beyond death. It occurs through Jesus Christ, not to deify man, but to rescue him from the sin against God and from the punishment of sin, namely death. Thus the death of Jesus protects against punishment in the judgment; God forgives man his self-glorification and leads him to eternal life for Jesus' sake. Christian salvation has nothing to do with reward as it is presented on the part of the Buddhists. In it, it is totally a matter of the restoration of the right relationship to God, of the new creation. *Soteria est recreatio.* The judgment is proof not only that man in his responsibility is taken seriously by God, but also that God's honor is upheld. In this judgment the verdict about the religions will also be given. They harden man in his opposition to God.

That becomes especially clear where the saving message of the Cross comes to man. Islam rejects the Son of God because it would be making God human to ascribe a son to him. It would be shameful if he allowed the Savior to suffer. It would be degradation of God if he could not be merciful without atonement. Hinduism and Buddhism understand the Cross only as a

symbol of the ultimate selfless response and reduce it to a moral.
The Buddhists are proud of needing no savior. The Hindus feel
it as an unreasonable demand to be expected to believe in a
savior. Salvation by grace is for both an abomination, although in
northern Buddhism and in the Bhakti religion in India, a doctrine
of grace is present. Neither, however, discards the transmigration
of souls, whereby the self-saving divine quality in man can increase from incarnation to incarnation. They acknowledge no
actual agent of salvation, because according to the Bhakti the
divine carries out salvation of itself, and in Buddhism Amida
Buddha is understood less as savior than as the incarnate Buddha
principle. In this sort of salvation no atonement, no forgiveness
of sins, no trust in God is needed. It is enough to release divine
dynamism in order to come under its effect.

The greatest offense remains this, that God has bound his saving will to Jesus Christ. Through him it becomes clear that the
non-Christian man, who remains far from God, also stands under
this saving will. God has allowed no other way to lead to him
except through Jesus Christ who is the way to the father. Through
him he has let it be proclaimed that no one can be saved without
repentance and forgiveness of sin. Thus Jesus becomes not only
the critic, but the end of all religions. There is no way around
him. In the rejection of the claim of salvation, the other religions
therefore turn themselves more and more into anti-Christian
religions. They reject the message of Jesus or wish to reshape it.
Thereby they overlook the fact that man can have neither Jesus
without the Gospel, nor the Gospel without Jesus. Both belong
together because he alone is the way, the truth, and the life.

7. THE NEW LIFE

Aside from this primary offense, the objections of the religions
against Christianity are based less upon philosophical than upon
ethical grounds. Since in them ethical behavior is a means of
salvation, their followers are filled with a great moral earnestness.
This position is encouraged today by nationalism, which gives the
peoples new tasks of unselfish effort. This results in a further

strengthening of the tradition by which the members of these peoples are carried along. It is, however, completely determined by religion and shapes the individual. Therefore the Asiatic people ask how it happens that Christianity has not succeeded in giving its people an ethical stability. They believe they find the answer in the fact that through the Christian doctrine of salvation, God's commandments have no place in life. Christianity announces salvation by grace, demands no ethical effort, and has little influence upon secular life; therefore, no ethical renewal proceeds from it. Where this doctrine is taken seriously, it results in an unworldly striving toward an everlasting bliss. Even where service is performed for the sake of the Lord, the ethical motive is not genuine. The morality of love becomes totally disrupted when it is combined with the idea of reward in heaven or in a later life, reward in the sense of eternal joy. This is transcendental other-worldly eudaemonism.[20] The Buddhists admit the egotistic motives in their own religion, however: "One may object here that even the overcoming of one's own suffering represents a selfish goal and that the striving for it moves along the line of an egoistic determination of one's goal."[21] That becomes especially clear in the presentation of Buddhism by Grimm, who describes the goal of salvation of Buddhism plainly as joy and happiness.[22]

Particularly in Buddhism, good does not occur for the sake of good, but is a part of the way of salvation because man will thereby move forward in freeing himself. Despite all self-confidence, he, too, is moved by the fear that he could sink lower in the next reincarnation. Good here serves the perfection of one's own self. Therefore the commands of Buddhism are always negatively determined, while the commands of God, Christian discipleship, are always related to this fellow man. The all-encompassing good always serves one's own person in Buddhism. How the Buddhist can be egotistic in the fulfillment of the commands, how he can pass by the suffering of his fellow man untouched, indeed

---

[20] Max Ladner, "Über die Nächstenliebe," *Einsicht*, 1956, p. 169.
[21] Ladner, "Buddhistische Moral," *Einsicht*, 1956, p. 142.
[22] George Grimm, *Das Glück, die Botschaft des Buddha* (1933).

can add suffering himself, we learn from the example of the monk who leaves wife and child in order to give himself over to meditation in the vicinity of Buddha. The wife seeks him out in her need, lays the child at his feet and says: "This is your son, Ascetic, feed him!" The monk, Sangamaji, does not bother himself about it at all. His wife goes forth horrified: "Even his son is of no importance to this ascetic." Buddha, however, praises this monk. He has cast off all ties. Here the ideal is serenity, indifference.

Christian love does not know this egoism. It does not offer itself for the sake of goodness, but for the sake of the Lord. It is not concerned with itself, but with the need of the neighbor. Nevertheless, we must accept a great deal that is said in those reproaches. It is actually true that we in Christianity have widely separated faith and life. The message of justification no longer has a place in life. One sees little evidence of the fact that the Christian is reborn and moves in a new life. The world sees and senses too little that Christians have the gift of the spirit of God. Above all, it hears too little of it! We preach the Word of God for itself, but no longer apply it to life. Out of fear of legalism and casuistry, we give up the law of God and forego giving the expectant a supporting idea and concrete guidance for their lives. The religions push into this vacuum and offer men a *philosophia perennis* by which they can shape their lives.

We must allow it to be said further in this connection: Men have had enough of always hearing about the sinner. Do not misunderstand me. As necessary as the recognition of sin and of the sinful being of man are for the comprehension of justification by grace, it cannot help the faithful to the joy of the saved sinner if the church shrinks from speaking of how he is set into a new life through the death and resurrection of Christ. How Paul makes the faithful joyous over justification! He speaks in the great indicative of what they have become through Jesus Christ. We rightly emphasize the *peccator*, but it is equally necessary to point to the *justus*, otherwise things progress to the place where men conclude that they remain *peccator*, the justification for sinning.

Let the same mind be in man that was in Jesus Christ! Men

should be able to see how the Christian message and the power of Christ determine the ethical life. The new life is a life through Christ. We can only be Christians insofar as we allow ourselves to be motivated by his love, insofar as he can achieve form in us. Then it will become clear: Whoever ventures life with Christ does not need the help of the other religions. Because, however, the old Adam is always more evident than the man of God in the life of Christianity, the non-Christians reject the Gospel today.

8. THE EQUALITY OF THE RELIGIONS

In the light of the Christian message, there is also another understanding of the religions and of Christianity. The thesis of the equality of the religions is justified insofar as without question Christianity is also a religion. Christianity is what men have made of the Gospel. It includes much more than the Gospel. When we speak of Christianity we mean the whole complex of the Christian cultus: Christian way of living, popular national organization, "Christian" culture and civilization, confessional and denominational disunion—all of nominal Christianity. That is something completely different from the Gospel, however. We should really have the courage, with Zinzendorf, to carry out this distinction completely. Only when we do that do we recognize our real task. We are not obligated to spread Christianity, but the Gospel. We do not have to christianize, but to missionize. We cannot oppose the foreign religions with Christianity, but only with the Gospel. The more we use this principle also for church work at home, the more fruitful this work will become. In the comparison of Gospel and Christianity two things always become clear: Christianity always lives from the Gospel. That is not to say that other factors are not also at work. However, *whatever in Christianity is really Christian, comes from the Gospel.* Second, *the Gospel is, however, always the critic of Christianity.* The more Christianity is brought under this standard, the more Christian life is able to develop.

Christianity as a religion has very much in common with the other religions, above all the *homo religiosus,* who also develops in Christianity. When we inquire after the essential core we find scarcely anything in common, because the Gospel is always in Christianity, and when we inquire for the message we find Christianity cannot be presented without the Gospel.[23] In it, it becomes clear that the religions are basically different. The religions discern this themselves and therefore emphasize the thesis of the sameness of the goal of all religions in order to ensure their existence. All lead, despite their differences, to the same goal of truth. From the point of view of the Gospel, however, the equality of the religions is given in a different sense. They are all expressions of the yearning for God and, at the same time, of the separation from God, ways of man who is detached from God. The message of the Gospel is completely separate from the pronouncements of these religions, for it is the message of the one God, who through Jesus Christ has already answered the yearning for God and has ended the separation from God. His loving will is so encompassing that the letter to the Colossians can say God has reconciled the whole world in Christ. Thus the Gospel leaves no room for the other religions.

But let us again consider the question: "If the religions say basically the same thing, then each religion must recognize itself again in the pronouncement of the others. At least parts of their pronouncements must be interchangeable."[24] We do not need to make this attempt, for this exchange does not exist. Whether we take the concept of God, which in Islam is exaggeratedly transcendent, which in Christianity is held to be too anthropomorphic according to the judgment of the others, which has in Hinduism evaporated into an active something and which has completely disappeared in Buddhism; or the concept of sin, which is understood in Christianity as a transgression against God which needs forgiveness, in Islam as a false conduct of man which the sinner himself can make right, in Hinduism as an error which can be corrected, and in Buddhism does not really exist—everywhere there is a different understanding. We can make no exchange.

[23] H. Frick, *The Gospel, Christianity and other Faiths*, trans. James Haire (Oxford: Blackwell, 1938).

[24] W. Freytag, *Das Rätsel der Religionen und die christliche Botschaft* (*"Gespräch"*; Wuppertal-Barmen: Jugenddienst Verlag, 1956), pp. 8–9.

It is the same with analogies. The supernatural birth of Christ brings a true Son of Man, that of Buddha brings a supernatural king's son, that of Krishna brings a god. Of Jesus alone can it be said, a man "as we are" (Heb. 4:15). One cannot speak of things in common. The non-Christian religions consciously deify even their gods. The God of the Bible is God without its being necessary that something be ascribed to him by man. Just as the whole teaching of salvation of the non-Christian religions is an expression of the yearning toward the "more," so also is their belief in God. Therefore these religions cannot in the final analysis use Jesus, for his becoming man is an acknowledgment of man on God's part. Here man must not deify himself; he is made true man again through salvation.

Because the differences are so great, Christianity—since it has the Gospel for its content—cannot assimilate the other religions or be perfected by them. It can, to be sure, everywhere take on a human dress; it must, however adjust itself again and again to the Gospel. It cannot therefore take from men the decision for Christ. One cannot prove this claim to exclusiveness philosophically; it is simply given with the Christian revelation. The proof of truth can always only be won in faith. The believer does not experience the truth of the Gospel by himself, but only in the fulfillment of faith itself. This faith arises everywhere the Gospel is proclaimed. Thus through the development of the church, the Word of God itself brings the proof of its rightness.

The confrontation with the non-Christian religions can only occur through the testimony of biblical truth. The philosophical confrontation, to be sure, performs a preparatory service. Kraemer's book is a clear proof of this, but in the final analysis he can only bear witness to the truth.[25] In this confrontation it becomes clear that the biblical message is never concerned about religion as a system, but always with the man who, caught in religion, must be called back to God. He must come within the sound of the proclamation, the witness of the truth, the message of justification.

[25] Kraemer, *loc. cit.*

Holsten sees this quite correctly.[26] The Gospel must be offered to man. Therefore in Holy Scripture no distinction is drawn between the biblical message and the message of the religions, but only between the people of God and the heathen, between the congregation of Christ and the unbelievers. The congregation as the carrier of the message should win the unbeliever, and in this way it comes to grips with his religion. Through its proclamation man is led to faith and thus recognizes the truth of biblical revelation. The recognition of this truth is always bound to the readiness for personal testing. If Hinduism and Buddhism can lay emphasis upon experience in the recognition of truth when they recommend their ways of salvation, then the Christian faith may likewise call upon this experience. The truth of Christian revelation is always recognized at the point where through faith a life relationship is given between God and man. "If any man's will is to do [the will of him who sent me], he will know whether the teaching is from God or whether I am speaking on my own authority" (John 7:17). Man is always called to decision by the message and through it he can recognize the truth.

9. THE THREE NECESSARY WAYS

If we survey the failure of Christianity and examine the reproaches of the other religions, we must come to the conclusion that the Gospel has, through the life of Christianity, become for many men unworthy of belief. From this follows the further conclusion that through the lives of Christians it can again become believable for the peoples. Three ways seem to me to be required to achieve this end:

(1) Men expect above all *the applied word* from Christians. The Asiatics sense better than we that the church as it has become no longer has a message in this confused world. It has an excellent theology, a theology even that explains away the message, limits it, centers it existentially upon man; but does it still have a message by which the congregation of Jesus can live, a message

---

[26] W. Holsten, *Das Kerygma und der Mensch: Einführung in die Religions- und Missionswissenschaft* (Munich: Chr. Kaiser, 1953).

for man in his concrete needs and temptations? It has a rich proclamation, but is it not a proclamation of itself for its own sake? Is it not far more a piece of the Christian cult than a *viva vox evangelii*? Do we still have a premonition of the fact that revelation exists only because God has created men whom he wishes to save? Can one indeed establish the truth which revelation contains if one does not constantly have the goal and purpose of revelation in mind? The church's lack of authority is evident in the fact that it no longer recognizes a prophetic use of the Word, but thinks it is enough if it preaches the truth which the Bible contains as faithfully as possible. It no longer dares, however, to say what these Biblical truths mean for actual life. As was said, the other religions break into these gaps. How would it be if the church were again to call injustice injustice and sin sin? What kind of revolutionary power would the Gospel be if the church itself were no longer afraid of its realization?

Men can expect a directing word from the church, by which God leads them spiritually. Where this direction is given, a large number of human problems are already ended. For their ethical life men also expect very definite advice which tells them what is right and what is wrong. In certain situations of life they also expect a comforting word. Can a church comfort, however, if it regards suffering itself as something which should not be? It no longer corresponds to our picture of man that man must suffer; therefore we no longer realize that in suffering a deeper sense of God is given. Men also expect a word of hope. Can a church, however, give hope if it lets the message of hope as it is given in the resurrection and through eschatology be taken from it? To be sure, we preach the Cross, but does this still have a meaning for men if they do not hear of the Resurrection? If death is the last word, the message of the Cross is worthless. Can we still preach hope if eschatology is limited to the existential, if we no longer see in it the goal of history into which our history also flows?

It is not here a question of changing the world. It will always remain an evil world. Everything depends upon our helping man to a new life in Christ, in which we give him the strengthening,

sustaining, and life-shaping Word. This Word is much more important than outward help. Are we in the church not about to
forget that man is a creature who can be addressed? Do we still
trust that the Word can lead men? The other religions today
know a great deal more about the meaning of the "message" for
men than we do. Man does not want solutions, but guidance as to
how he can meet his decisions himself.

(2) The world is crying out today for a model. It has come
to the depths of ruin through the failure of the white race to
furnish a model. *The lack of a model is most closely connected
with the lack of the Word.* Because we no longer have the Word,
we seek salvation in organizational, economic, and technical areas.
We think to be able to impress men by elevated living, but is that
still a Christian life? The Word always aims to be made concrete
in life. We wish to replace through neutral institutions that which
is lacking in the life of Christianity. We believe that social needs
can be removed with money and technique, as if men's happiness
were a simple affair! Happiness is always a very relative concept.
What man understands by happiness his religion tells him. The
man who is bound by religion sees in things which we connect
with the idea of happiness not only what makes life easier, but
also what undermines his humanity. Therefore he judges the
message of Christianity by the dangers which proceed from
Western civilization. He does not wish to have his humanity, his
salvation constantly placed in jeopardy by them. In contrast to
this civilization, he would like to see a life that is bound to Christ
and given form by Him. That is the decisive factor. Radhakrishnan
once said to a missionary: "When your Christ has not succeeded
in changing you into better men and women, is there any reason
to assume he would do it for us if we became Christians?"

The church does a great deal to help those who are deprived of
their social rights, to set right again the sins of men. Thank God
it becomes clear here that Christians vicariously bear the sins of
men and exercise love where hate was sown. But have we even
once asked ourselves whether this service, as great as it is, can
in the eyes of non-believers be more than an acknowledgment of

the sin? Does the church not let its service be much too strongly dictated by the sinful world instead of giving impetus toward a new way of life? Do we still dare to call men quite concretely to discipleship? How important that would be we can see in the fact that the church is growing today everywhere where the Gospel is evident in the life of the congregation. The message always desires to enter fully into the witness and become realized in him. At the same time the church will have to be aware that discipleship is neither a social nor a political program. It will also not give us any right to an optimistic judgment of the world. It is part of Christian realism to know that the church can never establish social justice and guarantee peace. Even so, the church has to announce the command of God and to sharpen the conscience of men. The church will have to suffer, because it lives in the world, even from that which the world does in failing to heed the command. It cannot keep silent, however, and must know that even the temptations belong to a true Christian existence. The Christian martyrs demanded no security for their existence. They submitted to force because they knew the Lord who can also use evil in his service. That not only comforted them, but precisely in the helplessness over against force they became the model that overcame the world in faith.

(3) Men expect further a *true brotherhood*. Here, too, the Christians have failed. They have not set themselves against the arrogance of race; they have not secured a true community of man. Brotherhood is not yet assured by the fact that I help the other person in Christian love or that I raise him socially. Brotherhood is an acknowledgment of the humanity of the other, is a personal participation. It is a sharing of life so that I enter the life of another and am not ashamed of him. Because the laws of society have been stronger than Christian love, no true brotherhood has come about. This exists only on the basis of forgiveness. Through it community arises among men and among the peoples. These have a great deal to forgive the white race. It is further clear, however, that these other peoples commit the same outrage which the white race has inflicted upon them. We, too, have much

to forgive, especially the lack of gratitude which has become the accompaniment of nationalism today. Ought we not to go first in forgiving? At this point it could be demonstrated that the message of Jesus has its place in life.

These three lines are interwoven. It may be that at one time this one, at another time that one must be emphasized. Only together do they comprise the Christian witness.

10. THE MEANING OF MISSION AND THE YOUNGER CHURCHES

What was said in the previous chapter applies to every Christian. We have only indicated where the beginnings must lie. The realization of those beginnings would be an encounter with the world religions, but would still not be a coming to terms. We have still not mentioned anything of the special service of the church over against them. The church owes these peoples the Gospel. Since today the church is present among the non-Christian peoples, this special service takes place in a double sense. In carrying out the mission command, the whole church has the message of salvation in Jesus Christ to bring to these people, and the younger churches which exist in the territory of these religions must come to terms with them in a completely unique way. Since today the church is attacked along the whole front by these religions, the contrast between the people of God and the non-Christians again becomes particularly clear. Above all, therefore, the church in this service must appear in the unity of the Body of Christ.

Without question the younger churches are most strongly involved. They must bear the attack, must allow themselves to be designated as the outposts of the hated white race. Next to the message of salvation, the church is today the greatest offense to the Asiatic peoples. Since the non-Christian religions have no organizational form of religion of their own, they cannot understand that Christians gather together in the church. By baptism, which draws the dividing line, church is already given. The universal salvation of God demands that those who believe and are baptized be collected in the congregation of God. Thus the

congregations become the upraised symbol among the non-
Christians that there is only one salvation. Because they are subject to their head, Jesus Christ, and can live only through him,
they must hold themselves in a position of exclusiveness in relation to the other religions. Christianity can be no parasitic plant
that hangs itself upon others. The demarcation from the other
religions is precisely a condition of the church's being able to
deliver its message.

The younger churches are constantly under attack today. In
this dangerous situation they cannot and may not respond in the
manner that the churches of Asia have done since the seventh
century. They withdrew into their shell, surrounded themselves
with the armor of tradition and scarcely noticed how life was
dying out in the shell. Even today one can hear the word of the
silent witness. There is only one help for the church in such a
situation: witnessing to the Gospel, or the mission. The church
is called to come to terms with its environment continuously.
Through its life in the congregations the church should make
clear to the surrounding world how a new life grows through the
Gospel which makes itself effective along the three lines indicated
above. Through the younger churches the Gospel can enter the
cultures of the other peoples and enrich them. If the congregations transplant the Gospel into life, they not only effect such a
contribution to culture, but they also become centers of attraction
in their environment. Men obtain the model that they seek and
they sense the power of faith which supports this life. That will
become clearer to the degree that the younger churches prove
themselves in temptation. They then reply to the attacks without
themselves having to become aggressive.

The universal will for salvation demands, however, that the
church as a whole proclaim the Gospel to the non-Christians. If
God has ventured to affirm this to men in his son Jesus Christ,
then his congregation must also affirm its mission to mankind. It
must know that it would not have the Gospel itself were that
Gospel not meant for all men. The mission is the strongest proof
that God is working even today through his son Jesus Christ in

his church and through it among the peoples. The more a church becomes aware of its mission from its Lord, the more it also learns that it can carry out the confrontation with the other religions only in offering the Gospel. Thus the mission itself becomes a great help to the church in countering these influences.

In this way the churches of the older Christianity will not be oppressed by the activity of the other religions, and the younger churches will not despair under the attacks, for in the mission of Christianity the essential unity of all Christians will be revealed and will lead to common action. In this the brotherhood of Christians, their mutual sympathy and participation, must be confirmed. In this connection the ecumenical movement is of great significance. While up to now the word "mission" has always carried the odium of a Western move toward expansion, the response of Christianity will today make it clear that mission is an important life function of the church. Within the bounds of the over-all task a larger role already falls today to the younger churches than to the older churches. We ought to know, however, that the younger churches cannot perform their service if they do not receive from the older churches the support they are entitled to expect from the members of the Body of Christ, and on the other hand we must ourselves recognize that our service in missions can only be carried out if it takes place in relation to the younger churches. They represent today the larger missionary potential in the confrontation.

Missionary work cannot be accomplished in a theoretical fashion. Theoretical confrontation can always only be a preparatory service which the witness must follow. In the mission it is not a question of proof of a better religion. It is a matter of witnessing to the living Christ so that he may find entrance among men. Men should be offered the salvation of God. This witness cannot be shifted to a neutral plane. It must be practiced both at home and abroad by believing men. The more naturally it is manifested in the life of men the more attractive it will be. That will be the case if Christians are again aware of their faith so that it is effective in their whole lives.

Therefore the witness in the territory of these religions can best be practiced by the younger churches. Their members do not first have to familiarize themselves with the thinking of the non-Christians. They know their questions and answers. The more the younger churches cast off everything foreign, the more they will fulfill this task. The more they are rooted in their homeland, the better they can carry out this service.

The missionary work of the older Christian churches is not at an end; it is really only now beginning! It is accomplished, to be sure, in another fashion than formerly. It can only adapt itself to what is already being carried on by the younger churches in their countries:

True missionary work can only be carried forward by those who were themselves shaped by the history and culture of the men there and who therefore in every fiber of their being participate in the confrontation of the unchangeable Christian message with the spiritual powers of their countries.[27]

If, however, the Western missionary worker thereby joins in true brotherhood with the younger churches, there remain for him such great tasks that he does not have to regret the change brought about by time.

Unless all indications are misleading, the great confrontations lie before us. In them the fate of Christianity will be decided by the missionary witness of the church. This is the only help, the only means, that God has given his church in the competition of the religions. Thus Christianity, the older at home and the younger abroad, can only be helped by growing together into one body and allowing themselves to be led to missionary service. The more the church accepts this help, the more it will receive the consolation that no power on earth can overcome the church until its Lord comes, in whom it believes, toward whom it hurries and whom it serves, and who as Lord of the world and of the church realizes his goal with the peoples.

[27] Günther Schulz, *Kein Platz mehr für Weisse: Das Dilemma der Mission* (Berlin: Käthe Vogt Verlag, 1958), p. 52.

Index

Abdul, Mohammed, 16
Al-Afghani, Djamal Al-Din, 16
Aga Khan, 117
Ahmad, Mirza Ghulam, 40, 41, 45, 89, 117
Ahmadiyya, 7, 9, 21, 23, 31, 40-41, 44, 51, 54, 61, 70, 79, 85, 89, 91, 117, 118, 123
  in America, 118
  in Europe, 118
Allah, 72, 91, 96, 116
Ambedkar, 112
anthroposophy, 101-2
apostasy, 49, 56
Arya Samaj, 15, 33-34, 108
asceticism, 82, 84, 87, 100
Asoka, 9, 110, 123
atheism, 100, 105
Aurobindo circles, 108-9
Aurobindo, Sri, 25, 70, 72, 78, 108-9, 137
awakening, religious, 1, 14-45, 99

Bab [Sayyid Ali Muhammad], 90
Bahai sect, 9, 54, 92, 106
Bahaullah, 106
Barth, Karl, 127
Bhagavad-Gita, 34
Bhakti religion, 104, 140
Blanke, Fritz, 104, 107
Blavatsky, Mme. H. P., 16
Brahma, 28, 35
Brahma Samaj, 15-16, 18, 22, 24, 35, 108
brotherhood of man, 91, 116, 149
Brunton, Paul, 43, 49, 50, 63, 67, 69, 71, 78, 84, 88, 137
Buddha, 8, 20, 30, 39, 40, 43, 47, 83, 86, 87, 95, 96, 124, 135, 136, 140, 145
Buddha Jubilee, 5, 8, 122
Buddhism, 4-5, 8-9, 16, 17, 19-20, 22-23, 27, 30-31, 36-37, 38,

43-44, 47, 49, 52, 57, 67, 69, 71, 73, 74-76, 79, 80-83, 85-87, 89, 90, 93, 95, 97, 102-3, 110-15, 120, 122-25, 129, 130-36, 139-41, 144, 146
  in Burma, 20, 22, 36, 111
  in Cambodia, 111
  in Ceylon, 8, 20, 22, 36, 111-14, 122
  in China, 30, 110, 123
  in France, 113
  in Germany, 5, 114
  in India, 20, 110-11
  in Indonesia, 112
  in Japan, 30, 110, 113, 123
  in Laos, 111
  Mahayana, 110
  missionary societies of, 16, 114
  Northern, 27, 30, 86, 136, 140
  in Siam (Thailand), 23, 82, 111
  in Southeast Asia, 20, 110
  Southern, 20, 22, 36, 110
  in the United States, 113
Buddhist World Council, 44, 114

castes, 15, 22, 24, 123; see also outcastes
Chaitanya, Sri Krishna, 4, 109
Christian Fellowship Sect, 101-2
Christian Science, 102
Christianity, viii, ix, 2, 10-13, 15-16, 18, 21, 25, 27, 28, 31, 35, 37-41, 43, 46-52, 57, 58, 60-62, 94, 96-98, 100, 101, 107, 108, 115, 116, 121, 136, 140-141, 143, 144, 146, 152
  encounter with non-Christian religions, 1, 17, 33-34, 35, 50-52, 55-57, 63, 109, 121, 140, 145-46, 152-53
  failure of, 50, 55-61, 108, 146
  as historical religion, 120-21, 128

intolerance in, 55
use of force by, 51, 121, 122
Christian church(es), 1, 12, 37,
    48-49, 52, 57, 58, 97, 99,
    147, 150, 153
Church of the New Dispensation,
    25
colonialism, 3, 11-12, 17, 30, 37,
    50, 52, 62, 121, 123
communism, 12, 56, 60, 100
Conference of the World Fellow-
    ship of Buddhists, 114
Congress of Religions (Chicago,
    1893), 7, 32, 108
Conze, Edward, 5, 113, 122
corpus islamicus, 37, 116
Council of Rangoon, 31
creation, 46, 127, 130-131, 134,
    138
Cross, the, 139-140, 147

Darul-Islam (House of Islam),
    44, 116
Dayananda, Sarasvati, 32, 33
deification of man, 135-138
democracy, 12, 54
dharma, 30, 75-76
Dharmapal, Anagarika, 16
Divine Life Society, 26, 105

ecumenical movement, 92, 152
equality of religions, 34, 38, 92,
    93, 98, 106, 109, 143-46
Essenes, 39
ethic, 47, 80-85, 129, 140-43,
    148-50
    Buddhist, 47, 80-83, 141-42
    Christian, 129, 141, 148-50
    Hindu, 83-84
    Islamic, 84-85
evil, doctrine of, 68-70, 134

faith, 49-50, 66, 130-31, 142,
    145-46
Farquhar, John N., 24
fatalism, 29, 133
forgiveness, 34, 46, 134
freedom, fight for, 29, 34
freedom of man, 131-132

Gandhi, Mahatma, 4, 7, 8, 24, 29,
    30, 34, 35, 39, 40, 42, 57, 83,
    91, 108, 122
Gaudiya Mission, 109
Germany, 10, 99, 102, 103, 113,
    114, 118
Ghana, Mission Conference in,
    36-37, 52
Gnosticism, 40, 101
God, doctrine of, 73-80, 126-31;
    see also monotheism, Trinity
    Buddhist, 74-76
    as emanation, 48
    Hindu, 76-79
    Islamic, 79-80
    as person, 24, 25, 33, 46, 47,
    120
Gospel, viii, ix, 15, 19, 38, 40, 41,
    50, 51, 55, 58, 60, 62, 63, 95,
    101, 125, 128-129, 140, 143,
    144-47, 150-53
Grimm, George, 141

Hecker, Hellmuth, 91
Herbert, Jean, 104
Hinduism, 4, 7-8, 15-16, 18-19,
    20, 22, 23-26, 28-30, 32-36,
    38, 39-40, 42-43, 47, 52, 65,
    66, 68-69, 71, 73, 76-79, 83-
    84, 85, 87-89, 90, 91, 93, 96,
    97, 112, 117, 120, 122, 123,
    124, 125, 129-31, 133, 135,
    139, 140, 144, 146

Type used in this book
Body, 10 on 13 and 9 on 12 Caledonia
Display, Spartan
Paper: White Standard Antique "R"